VETTIUS VALENS

of Antioch

4.1

Rendered from ancient Greek

into modern English

by

Andrea L. Gehrz

Moira Press

Portland, OR

Copyright © 2017 by the Moira Press

Translator: Andrea L. Gehrz
Cover Design: Andrea L. Gehrz
Edited by: Sara Beth Brooks

Published by Moira Press
www.moirapress.com

ISBN 978-0-9987015-1-6

Note: *All Greek words in the footnotes are directly cited from the:*

Liddell & Scott:
Greek-to-English Lexicon.

Table of Contents

a; The Division of Periods

It seems the appropriate time to facilitate a fitting and didactic release of previous topics upon which to feast the mind. The division of life into practical and impractical times is a topic of frequent inquiry; one which has remained elusive thus far. I will now show through examination and analysis the extent to which these divisions have been made clear. Most directly, the first period is taken from a one-quarter calculation of the star's minimal period.

For instance, **Saturn** has a minimal period of 30 years. One-quarter of 30 years is 7 1/2 years.

This number has also been cast out by the year to find a daily ratio, 85.

Jupiter's cycle is 12 years. One-fourth of this is three years. Extrapolated to days of year, 34.

Mars has a period of 15 years.

One-quarter of this is 3 years 9 months.

In yearly days, this becomes 42 1/2.

Venus has a period of 8 years, one-quarter of which is 2 years. The yearly days are 22 2/3.

Mercury has a period of 20 years.

One-quarter of this is 5 years.

Yearly days are 56 2/3.

Sun is 19 years.

One-quarter of this is 4 years, 9 months.

And in days, 53 1/2.

Moon is 25 years, one-quarter of which is 6 years, 3 months. Yearly days are 70 1/3.

From which we get 32 years, 3 months.

β; On Aphesis

We shall now address the reckoning of the vital quadrant through the release of counting from a certain star; the process of *Aphesis*[1]. In new moon charts, the counting begins at the new moon region, proceeding in succession. In full moon charts, the counting begins at the full moon and progresses from there.

A synthesized account of the star:

How it is configured? Is it witnessed by other stars? How is it receiving other stars? Is it on a pivot? Has it already declined? Is it rising near the east or setting near the west? Will its trek create sympathies or antipathies?

When the count reaches 32 years & 3 months, we must make a second circle from the square side of the aphetic star.

---

[1] *Aphesis* = A letting go, release.

The starting point of horses in a race.
The actual starting post.

In astrology = the reckoning of the vital quadrant (288).

γ; On the Finer Division of Days

Let's create a finer division in terms of days. Suppose Saturn is the general aphetic star. Saturn is allotted 7 1/2 years. Suppose we extrapolate this number to all stars. From this calculation, a finer division is derived. In multiplying the 85 days of Saturn by 7 1/2, we get 637 1/2. We then use this number to discover the finer allotments for Saturn by its own years, 7 1/2. Let's now look to Jupiter. Since it governs 34 days, we multiply this number by 7 1/2, as Saturn is the general aphetic star. We arrive at a total of 255. This will be Jupiter's number per Saturn. Next, we take Venus. She is said to rule 32 2/3 days. Multiplied by 7 1/2, the total becomes 170. This is the number of days for Venus—per Saturn. We apply this process to each star; multiplying each set of days by 7 1/2. From this calculation we discover the finer division of days.

If somehow the Moon is governing aphesis, then each set of days is multiplied by 6 1/4 years to show the appropriate number.

Discovering the Days for Each Star

The initial days of each star have been discovered in this manner. The planetary period has been multiplied by two, divided in half, and divided by one-third. These have been added together.

For instance, the period of Saturn is 30 days. Multiplied by 2, this becomes 60. Divided in half it becomes 15. One-third of 30 is 10. The total of 60, 15, and 10, is 85. These are the days of Saturn.

The process is similar for the remaining stars.

δ; On the Distribution of Time Periods from the Lots of Fortune and Spirit

Now, I shall establish a powerful teaching.

This technique is to begin reckoning the vital quadrant from the lots of fortune and spirit, which signify Sun and Moon. Within the cosmic arrangement, the Moon lies in close proximity to earth. Through her adjacency, the Moon affects body and breathe, streaming downward and escorting us into manifestations of various kinds. The Moon is literally the governing force of the body that has come along with us. Moreover, the Sun has its own divine action; to enliven the mind to its perceptive capabilities — memory, recall, reasoning, and intellect. The Sun also lights up individual destiny through the *daimon*[2]. Moreover, the Sun's nature is beautiful and pleasant.

---

[2] *Daimon* = God, goddess of an individual (366)
Divine power controlling the destiny of individuals.

The Sun directly awakens the soul and contributes a unique style of movement responsible for the praxis taken up. When we inquire into bodily periods (climaxes, weakness, bloodshed, calamity, sickness, pathology, strength, pleasure, enjoyment through beauty, or engagement in aphrodisial affairs, and all else that might happen to the physical vessel) we must cast out by sign from the lot of fortune, until the counting stops. Here, we reckon the sign, any stars on it, and angles to it.

How is this region configured to the general chart or to the ruler of the aphetic period? Are the *time rulers (chronocraters)* of the lots on pivots or out of the pivots[3]? If we inquire into praxis or reputation, we release the time periods by sign, from spirit. Examine anything on these places, or angles to them (benefic or malefic) and make a determination from there.

---

[3] *Chronocrators* = literally.....time-rulers (2008).
A heavenly body that dominates for a time period.

Often, the lot of fortune or its ruler have fallen aside. The lot of spirit is allotted to both bodily and practical matters. Similarly, luck is allotted to both fortune and spirit. In terms of ultimate rulership and house rulership, a ruler might be cast aside. When spirit and fortune are in the same sign, bodily matters are taken from that sign. Practical matters are apprehended from the region rising up to the ascendant.

Now, let's consider new moon and full moon charts found to have the same aphesis, especially with fortune and spirit presenting in the same sign. When we inquire into bodily periods with placements such as these, we release counting from the same sign. The practical affairs are reckoned from the sign rising to the lot. Especially in night charts, when the new moon has come to a position under the earth, configured at the pivot square to each lot. This class of new moon charts are stronger than those of the full moon. Observe that a new moon chart will have both lots on the ascendant. Full moon charts will have one lot setting. And the lots often come together, square to the lights, which are opposite themselves.

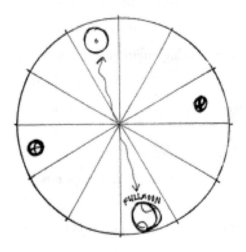

In this image, certain things are allotted to occur in practical periods, as taken from the ascension of signs. Yet, this does not seem correct to me. This is because fortune and spirit are to be discovered in both new moon and full moon charts. Another consideration is that more often in charts of males, the counting is released from spirit; because the male praxis involves the logic of giving and receiving. Males often pursue an art driven by a belief in the work. In charts of females, the counting is often released from fortune, as there is an occupation with bodily matters. Men also walk through bodily matters, leading to practical tasks requiring the use of their hands — athletics, and other movement-oriented jobs. Females gravitate towards purchasing and sales. Moreover, in the charts of infants, we release the times from fortune up to the testing period at the acme of existence. By this time, a person will have matured into their specific praxis. When one has arrived at this period, they spend their days cheerfully, enjoying good luck with bodily affairs, a beautiful form, elegance, daintiness, a rhythmic cadence, and all other things that resemble this period; sickness, pathology, eczema, expulsions, ulcers, hernias, anything signified in the genesis. Practical and intellectual considerations follow.

Let us look to an example where both fortune and spirit reside in Aries. The general ruler is Mars. The lots are combined by house and configured in an unnatural place. First, allot 15 years, from which we can also derive a finer division of 15 months. Next allot 8 months for Venus, via Taurus.

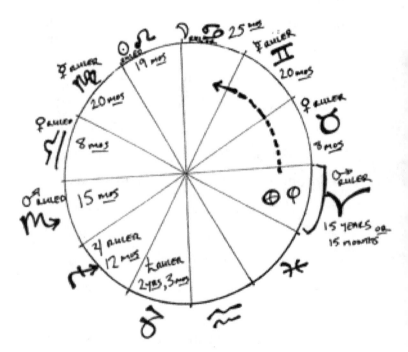

Then 20 months for Mercury per Gemini, 25 months for the Moon per Cancer, and 19 months for the Sun per Leo. Allot 20 months for Mercury, 8 months for Venus, and Mars, in its own sign, via the Scorpion, 15 months. Then Jupiter, 12 months by Sagittarius and Saturn by Capricorn, 2 years and 3 months. The remaining 11 in the filling up of 15 years occur in Aquarius.

Venus will take over for Mars on the eighth year; acquiring the general time periods. Next, we take the finer divisions into each sign, as set out before. Mercury will take over from Venus, via the 20 years of Gemini, and the finer divisions of each sign. Then, the Moon 25 years and Sun 19 years. Depending on the nature of the genesis, we must give the appropriate number to each sign in succession. The circle of 12 signs leads to 17 years and 7 months. And thus, we allot the remaining times from the diameter. For instance, since Gemini is allotted 20 years, the counting will be made in succession, filling 17 years and 7 months, with 2 years and 5 months remaining from Sagittarius. Giving the year to the same sign of Sagittarius, the remaining time will increase 20 years because of Capricorn.

We count similarly from:

Cancer, Leo, Virgo, Capricorn, or Aquarius.

Authors on the subject have separated the counting at the diameter, at 17 years and 7 months, allotting the remaining times in succession. Some have allotted the remaining times from the triangles. This does not seem natural to me. Consider that the four elements of the cosmos seem to exist in order to provide sympathies with one another. Each element is warmed and propagated by another. In a similar way, harmony can be fostered during finer divisions of time, as the stars make their transfers. For instance, fire and air are both carried upwards, heartily mixing and mingling. But fire on its own is dry, stale, parched, etc. Fire is nourished by a beneficial mixing with air. Fire is intrinsically unlike air, inasmuch as air is icy-cold and dark. Yet, fire can thoroughly furnish works through this beneficial mixing, and the warmth it emanates. It seems good logic to say that the Lion exists, within the circle of time, to be fiery in nature; handing over the remaining time to the sympathetic air sign of Aquarius and conversely, Aquarius to Leo. Maintaining this logic, earth is dry; nourished and propagated in all ways by water. The same is true of water, which can be weighed against earth. Water is protected by the sympathetic quality of all created by earth. It is good logic to say Cancer exists to be very watery. Capricorn, to be earthy. They mutually accommodate one another. Equivalently, Virgo is earthy, accommodating Pisces. The remaining signs hold similar potentials throughout, in how they interact with one another and their opposite signs. This consistent system can be applied to the entire distribution of twelve signs, making a chart of the elements.

Example:

Aries the Ram	Fiery
Taurus the Bull	Earthy
Gemini the Twins	Airy
Cancer the Crab	Watery

This pattern of elements continues through the four triangles. If we loosen the bonds in the triangles, we discover one nature in the sign giving over, and another in the sign receiving the transfer. Through this process, we don't always discover a harmonious combination. At times, there is an excess of some element through the mixing. Also, we can notice the Sun, beginning its yearly turn in Aries, continuing through the equinoxes, lays down a hemicircle as it begins increasing the magnitude of days. The Sun loosens its bonds into the diameter of Aries, which is Libra. Libra is the point where the Sun separates from its beginning, and the length of daylight begins to decrease. Cancer is a point in the circular schema when the length of days are increasing. Sun in Capricorn provides a nighttime correlation, creating a change in the airs at the diameter. The Moon, in making herself new, fills up the circle until the diameter; where she loosens her bonds. Because of this, it seems better to utilize the preceding teaching about the loosening of the bonds.

ε; On the Loosening of Bonds and Mutual Accommodation of Stars

There will be variances in the loosening of the bonds, as each star has its own unique nature. For instance, in terms of the yearly cycle, the Sun and Moon transfer over to Saturn. Clearly, fear is associated with this transfer. Saturn periods lead to greater enmity, mysterious threats through ancient matters, ravaging judgements, harsh confrontations, suspicious yet worthy lifestyles and values, the pulling down of the body through annoyances, danger, sudden, and unforeseen circumstances, home-coming by sea, and great responsibilities. Unless of course benefics are on this region or witnessing it. In this case, the benefics obscure any hindrance of responsibilities.

A transfer from Mercury to Jupiter (from Virgo or Gemini) will change the nature of the time period, manifesting the pragmatic affairs fully, making the praxis commonly known to many. If these regions are maltreated in the natal chart, or if Mercury is itself maltreated, the time will be generally oppositional. In this case, the loosening of bonds will positively change the ethers, bringing more strength, success in practical matters, etc. If these places are occupied by benefics, outcomes during this period will also be beneficial. Loosening of the bonds can bring disturbances and punishment. Saturn, because of Capricorn and Aquarius, will loosen its bonds into Leo and Cancer, indicating practical times. This transfer delivers darkness into light. The time will turn over to powerful signs, bringing a highly active state during the transfer. The exact nature will depend on the quality of foundation at genesis. Good public reputation and assistance will be provided, the nature of which will depend on the exact stars in these places.

ς; The Number of Years Allotted to Each Sign
And the Manifestation Years of Stars

Aquarius has been allotted 30 years. Capricorn has been given 27 years. The Sun governs 120 manifestation years; half of which is 60. Half of this number provides the allotment to Aquarius; 30 years. This is because of the diameter to Leo. The Moon governs 108 manifestation years; half of which is 54. Half of this number provides the allotment to Capricorn; 27 years. The remaining stars receive the finer division of manifestation years from Sun and Moon. Jupiter shares its class with Sun. It provides sympathy by triplicity via Sagittarius. The Sun allotted half of its 120 years, added to the minimal years of 19 — becomes 79. In this way the Moon shares a cosmic sympathy with Pisces (and Jupiter) by triplicity. Because it creates good things, it has been allotted half of 108 years (54), plus its minimal years of 25. This becomes 79.

Mars, same class as the Moon, has been allotted 54 years. The Sun is fiery, a close imitation to Mars. Its nature can cause deterioration, etc. It is denied finer allotment. In return, Jupiter furnishes because of its successorship in triplicity rulership. It has been given an allotment of a minimal finer division of 12. This becomes 66. Moreover, Venus has a sympathetic quality by triplicity and shares in the nighttime class with the Moon. The Moon has a finer division of 54. Saturn, because of the opposition to its exaltation in Libra, is 30 years. This becomes 84. Mercury shares house rulership to Saturn, and is taken according to this, providing 57 manifestation years and 19 minimal years by the Sun. This becomes 76.

ζ; A Division of Time Periods by the Lots of Fortune and Spirit

Also, the Trampling of Stars, Housemasters, the New Moon Place, Full Moon Place, and Mutual Accommodation

Examples Included

Now, we must observe the distribution of times in terms of the star handing over and the one receiving the transfer. Does the transfer occur on a pivot? A region that has declined? Regions agreeable in nature? Foreign? If the distribution by sign is from a pivot to a pivot, and the rulers of these pivots are also on pivots, witnessed by benefics, at home by sect, the time-rulership will offer a wonderful quality; delivering positive, significant manifestations. If the regions of transfer are pivots, but the rulers have declined, under rays of a malefic, etc., the time period will be confusing and anomalous.

If the entire schematic is configured in cadent houses the period will be worse; bringing blame and punishments. The practical affairs will change during the transfer of times; the focus turning to foreignness. If benefics are involved, or aspects from benefics, upright and practical affairs will occur on foreign soil; there will be aid. If malefics are involved, entrapments will occur in foreign countries. This could manifest as upheaval, punishment, etc. Or, the native could be abandoned by foreign people or slaves. Cadent houses signify foreign things. If the transfer occurs on pivots and the stars are in their own places, this can signify life in certain locations, or tarrying there. Neither Mercury nor Venus provide much time abroad, as they stay quite close to the Sun. Saturn, Mars, and the Moon bring banishment and danger by earth and sea, in places of wandering, and by barbarians. The Sun brings honor, esteem, and consistency. Jupiter offers love, aid, and pleasure in foreign lands. If the star ruling the bodily period is not on a pivot, it will bring down the sign. If its ruler is also not near the pivots, witnessed by malefics, there will be weakness, bloodshed, and danger. If the star drawing down the time period, according to spirit, is in a sign not near the pivots, and a malefic is on it, the sign's ruler also witnessing, the period will be impractical; passing in an unlucky manner. In this case, there will be an anarchy of spirit, creating a mean time for practical affairs and every thing cast in the chart. If the star is found in a fiery sign, the time brought down by malefics or their witnessing, will initiate a great feebleness of spirit. A veering off course will occur. Some things will be accomplished with great instability of thought and opinion. If air, with a maltreated sign or ruler, time will pass as the native rises up through great grief; fulfilling the expectations of another. If an earth sign, events encountered will be embraced due to the birth nature. Through great self-mastery, control, and personal invention, he will be surrounded by greatness. If in a watery sign, things acquired will easily console the spirit.

η; A Necessary Example

Let us look to a sample genesis containing these indications.

Pisces Rising
Sun and Venus in Cancer
Moon in Pisces
Mercury in Leo
Mars in Scorpio
Jupiter in Capricorn
Saturn in Sagittarius
Full Moon in Sagittarius
Lot of Fortune in Leo
Spirit in Scorpio

I inquire about the 70th year. I release the counting of bodily periods from Leo. I give the first sign of Leo 19 years. Next, 20 years for Virgo, 9 years for Libra, and 15 years for Scorpio.

The total becomes 62 years.

In this span, there are many climaxes; falls from high places, slaughtering of limbs, etc. Next, 8 years remain from Sagittarius, where Saturn is lying, not within the chart's class. In these years, the native survived shipwreck and physical disturbance.

Let us now observe the specific pathologies brought about by each sign. Look to the ruler of fortune to see what sign it is traveling through and discover possible maladies from this sign. Suppose the lot is in Leo. The ruler of the Lion is the Sun; residing in Cancer. Cancer signifies the breasts and stomach. We might now say, that this genesis is responsible for the pathologies of *Cancer the Crab*.

The finer divisions of time, in years, are created from the circle of 360 days. Each year has 5 1/4 extra days. Let's give Sagittarius 1 year. Capricorn, 2 years & 3 months. Aquarius, 2 years, 6 months. Pisces, 1 year. The remaining portion, in the filling up of 9 years, is given to Aries. Mars is the ruler of the bodily periods from Sagittarius. Saturn in Sagittarius is also considered to be leading the manifestation of ultimate life destiny—or *telos*[4].

---

[4] *telos* = fulfillment, execution, life outcome (1772)

The years of life were proved beforehand. The prognosis was stomach illness and cough. The place of death is housed by Pisces; the Moon lying on it, with Saturn in a superior square. This is quite powerful. Also, Saturn governing the full moon region, is turned away in the formation, which contributes to violent death. The stomach illness and cough was indicated by the ruler of fortune; Sun in Cancer. The Crab indicates the breast, chest, and stomach. The practical times were created from Scorpio, giving it the same years as Mars (15), then 12 for Sagittarius, as Saturn is lying in Sagittarius. There was anomalous wandering until the age of 27. Expenditures came under guardianship, yet the life was sufficient. The place of accumulation and preservation is Gemini. None of the benefics are looking to it. Only Saturn is opposed. Next, Capricorn takes over for 27 years. Jupiter is lying on the place of good spirit (11th House), rising at sunset under the Sun, in the gaze of Venus.

The entire time-graph is concerned with practical things; popular affairs, leadership, royal beliefs, friendliness with royalty, and abundant, suitable resources. Oppositions and anomalies will occur according to each critical time, season, and opportunity *(kairos)*. Yet, there can be survival through reception by malefics and the angles made by them. Resources acquired will be transient because of Jupiter being retrograde; in its fall. After Capricorn, the time is taken over by Aquarius. Mars and Mercury are witnessed by benefics, in aversion. The native stopped the practical works, turning far away from tasks previously believed in. The native took his hand to domestic affairs, beliefs, and slaves, from which a harsh and cruel quality prevailed; scarcity, debts owed to those in proximity, and eventual escape. Things materialized this way due to the general nature of the foundation chart.

The calculation is as follows;

Aquarius, 2 years 6 months. Jupiter, 1 year.
Mars, 1 year 3 months. Venus, 9 months.
Mercury, 1 year 8 months.

Apart from a general waning, there was room for many pragmatic affairs.

The Moon takes over next for 2 years 1 month.

In this period, things understood before seemed to end. The native helped loved ones make art.

The Sun takes over for 1 year & 7 months, per Leo. Then Mercury takes over for 1 year and 8 months, via Virgo. These places, witnessed by malefics, were diminished during the Mercury period. The lot has declined. The triplicity ruler of the Moon is Mars. Venus is taken with Mercury for 8 months. Then, Mars takes over for 1 year and 3 months, and Sagittarius for 1 year. This unfolding created the *telos*[5].

----

[5] For more information on *telos*, see *"An Introduction to Teleology for the Modern Astrologer"* at .astro.com

θ; On the Cosmic Year, And the Year's Distribution

Also, the Quantity of Each Star in Days, & How to Calculate this Number

The cosmic year is 365 and 1/4 days. Distributing to year 37. Remove 5 and 1/4 from each year. Make a sum total of years, then make the distribution. Let's make this calculation against the preceding genesis. Suppose something occurs in the 33rd year that brings about struggle. Birth occurred on 15 Tybi. The inquiry is for the 33rd year, Mesore 20. Multiply 30 years times 5. This becomes 150. Two full cycles means we add 10. And then, one-quarter of 32, which is 8. Our current total is 168. Take this from the 15th day of Tybi to the day of inquiry, Mesore 20. This becomes 215. Add this to 168 for a total of 383. Subtract 360 from this number.

$$383 - 360 = 23$$

According to this distribution, the genesis will be brought down at 33 years and 33 days. Count the time periods out this many years and days.

ι; Allotment of Years, Months, & Days, Great Periods and Lesser Periods, And the Hours of Each Star

Also, the Usefulness of these Calculations in the Nativity

We know the exact calculation of each period by taking the years divided by 12. Through this calculation, we find the number of days allotted to each star. For instance, Aries is given 15 years; divide this by 12, which gives 15 months. 1/12 of 15 months, is 37 and 1/2 days. 1/12 of this, is 3 days and 3 hours. These quantities are allotted by casting them out in time. Finer distributions of the remaining stars are discovered similarly. For instance, if a star has a certain distribution in the general time period, it can also be examined by its yearly ratio, monthly increment, number of days, and hours. We can set up even finer divisions, casting out by each star, to see what the native might encounter.

Sun is 19 years, 19 months, 47 1/2 days, 3 days and 23 hours. Moon is 25 years, 25 months, 62 1/2 days, 5 days, and 5 hours. Saturn is 30 years, 30 months, 75 days, 6 days, and 6 hours. Capricorn is 27 years, 27 months, 67 1/2 days, 5 days, and 15 hours. Jupiter is 12 years, 12 months, 30 days, 2 days, and 12 hours. Mars is 15 years, 15 months, 37 1/2 days, 3 days, and 3 hours. Venus is 8 years, 8 months, 20 days, 1 day, and 16 hours. Mercury is 20 years, 20 months, 50 days, 4 days, and 4 hours.

☉ SUN	☽ MOON	♄ SATURN	♂ CAPRICORN
19 YEARS	25 YEARS	30 YEARS	27 YEARS
19 MONTHS	25 MONTHS	30 MONTHS	27 MONTHS
47½ DAYS	62½ DAYS	75 DAYS	67½ DAYS
3 DAYS,	5 DAYS,	6 DAYS,	5 DAYS,
23 HOURS	5 HOURS	6 HOURS	15 HOURS
♃ JUPITER	♂ MARS	♀ VENUS	☿ MERCURY
12 YEARS	15 YEARS	8 YEARS	20 YEARS
12 MONTHS	15 MONTHS	8 MONTHS	20 MONTHS
30 DAYS	37½ DAYS	20 DAYS	50 DAYS
2 DAYS,	3 DAYS,	1 DAY,	4 DAYS,
12 HOURS	3 HOURS	16 HOURS	4 HOURS

Suppose we discover a genesis at 50 or 60 years. We make the counting of years from fortune or spirit by sign, giving each period the number of years it is able to hear. Next we allot months, days, then hours. If examining the chart of an infant, we count first by hours, then days, then months.

Let us now rejoice in a sample chart.

Leo Rising
Sun and Mercury in Capricorn
Jupiter and Saturn in Leo
Venus and Mars in Aquarius
Moon in Gemini
Lot of Fortune in Pisces
Lot of Spirit in Capricorn

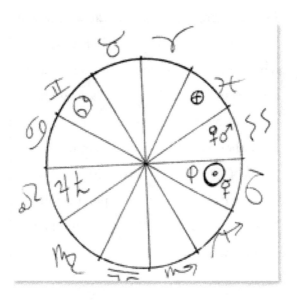

In this chart, the counting of times begins from the lot of fortune, in Pisces. The inquiry examines the 5 1/4 days of the year at Mesore. There has not yet been an allotment of 12 to Pisces. Give 12 months to Pisces, then 1 year and 3 months to Aries, and 8 months to Taurus. This gives us a total of 2 years and 11 months. Next, Mercury is given 1 year and 8 months, up to the filling up of 1/4 years and 7 months. The chart has not yet completed this period of years. Let the time-ruler be Mercury, which already has 9 months and 15 days. This is a total of 255 days. Allot this number through the signs in succession. Take Mercury first, as it correlates to Gemini; 50 days. Next, Cancer is given 62 1/2 days, then Leo 47 1/2 days, Virgo 50, and Libra 20 days. Our total is now 230. 25 days remain. Mars will take these in Scorpio, from the days of Venus up to 37 1/2. 25 days is the allotment to Mars, and so on.

First, it gets 3 days and 3 hours, then Sagittarius 2 1/2 days, Capricorn 5 days and 15 hours, Aquarius 6 days and 6 hours, then Pisces 2 1/2 days. Aries 3 days and 30 hours. Taurus participates in the filling up, with 25 remaining days. The general time-ruler is Jupiter. Mercury takes over, second from Jupiter. Third is Mars from Mercury. Fourth is Venus from Mars.

Observe these increments of the nativity to see their indications and if they are somehow configured to one another.

Some authors have allotted finer divisions of days according to triplicities. In some charts, the general time-ruler is found to be a benefic. The Sun and Moon have acquired resources — good reputation, leadership abilities, notable beginnings, help, and commendations by great people. If, according to the distribution of times, a malefic takes over in a certain period, the body will be weakened during the finer division.

There will be danger around the day of the transfer. When in opposition to the general time-ruler, or configured unsuitably by house, according to genesis, the road will lead to upheaval. Life will be equipped for fearful situations and punishment. If the general time-ruler is poorly placed in the natal chart, in the gaze of malefics, expect situations in the days of the finer divisions that bring danger, oppositions, etc. If the general time-ruler takes over during a period, in productive signs, witnessed by benefics on the roadway around, annoyances in life and reputation may surface, yet everything will remain in tact, enduring and strong. In the daily distribution of times, loosen the bonds when the circle fills up with 528 remaining. Release the counting in the opposite position and in succession throughout. When filling up the finer portions of days and hours, and 44 days remain in the circle, release the counting from the diameter in succession throughout.

ια; Productivity of the Year, And a Teaching by Parts

The general chronological distribution has been set up by house. Now, it's time to discuss productivity of the year and all that comes along with it. A few things have been mentioned earlier on the topic, drawn out and delineated as necessary. Many authors have put forth this time distribution in a confusing manner. Those setting up the times without any truth have handed over the techniques in a way so as to create ill will around them. And yet, there are enough teachings hidden away, discovered through much wandering, to provide an eternal quest for those who happen upon them. Some come to the study without any experience. Because of the particular subject matter, false lines of thinking do exist, calculated with tactics to deceive. Others have seen its potential to be highly useful and pragmatic. These are people who have set out to begin counting through the times, devoid of any ill-will.

Some of us have marched through various regions, passed through the teachings of Egypt, and are now surrounded by those who love money. We can create useful gifts from the study; fulfilling people's needs through a burning desire for the work. If we come across something that seems untrue, we can exercise self-control. We can take up the study with self-sufficiency, occupying ourselves with other endeavors in such moments. The vastness and mathematics of the study does present problems of course; as does the distribution of times in general. Thus, we may find ourselves pulled in many different directions. Yet, from a passion that burns within, we can construct something better; accepting loyalty to the study as a personal fate. Slander and accusations of fraud do arise regarding the general divisions of time, because some use bounds to find general rulership, others use micro-periods, and others use the twelfth-part of the *dodekata-moria*, adding up in increments of 10 years, 9 months[6], and so on. Some have even used exaltations for the finer divisions, signifying a false disembarking. Personally, it seems much worse to me to delineate the years of manifestation by 2, 10, or 7. Instead, we should

---

[6] *dodekatamoria* = twelfth part, sign of the zodiac (464)

inquire into the portions allotted within the yearly periods. And no matter how much time we carry across in releasing the counting throughout, there are those who make changes to the places as well. For those who are quite eager toward such things, we have experimented with various techniques by mixing them together, clear up through the place of spirit. Some individuals have wished for a specific manifestation because of intuition, and thus, have made the transfer into a certain place. Individuals who have begun their introduction with hard work and great toil, comprehending that which their eye fixes upon, putting their mind on this introduction, will surely notice its veritable powers and good uses. In practicing our daily business, engaging with various people, and seeing certain pathologies with our own eyes, we can parcel out a most holy, immortalizing viewing of the subject. We can impart this knowledge bountifully; offering chapter headings of the most essential and gripping parts of the doctrine. For without a process such as this, not one thing in existence would survive in the first place.

True manifestation begins with foresight.

I now administer an oath, celebrating these sacred rites for my most honorable brothers; becoming initiates by way of this collection on the heavens — the starry vessel, twelve portions, Sun, Moon, and five wandering stars. All life is guided through the outer forces, much like the sacred, holy, fated quality of *pronoia*[7]. May we preserve, protect, and conceal these concepts, not sharing them with the uneducated and uninitiated. May we also aim to share the most worthy powers and potentials of this study. Having shared these concepts righteously, please also impart a good mention of me, Vettius Valens. This will certainly allow an everlasting remembrance of my contribution; the fact that I have introduced new concepts, customs, and a bountiful comprehension, focusing on the parts that seem most true. A man working under no one; set free and truly illuminated. Of course, my name need not be presented to all who come upon this collection. At least they won't plagiarize or speak erroneously of things to come, bringing rejection

---

[7] *Pronoia* = perceiving beforehand, foresight, foreknowledge, divine providence (1491)

and adding blemish to my name. These things the gods have said beforehand shall be thoroughly guarded with goodwill and favor by all. In this way, life can come together and manifest in a stable, tranquil manner; following the logic of what is shown to the mind and lies heavy on the heart. Yet, may turbulence befall those who falsely swear on this oath. May they not walk successfully along the earth, sail the sea, or sow the seeds of children. They are blind inasmuch as the mind is fettered. In this way, they will be lead to a troubled existence, missing the mark of good things. Whether one is to be compensated after death with hostile or beautiful immortality, will depend on the partaking of similar things during the life time. If one has come to this point in these teachings, and after thoroughly learning the techniques, discovers an enigmatic part in another collection, they need not depart from praise. Instead, they can rejoice over the similarities in logic, noticing that the study offers not only predictions. There exist many other discoveries to add to this honorable school of thought. Many will take up parts of this collection bountifully and without envy, even if collected in malice. I am especially compelled towards the gems I have personally uncovered in this collection. Through these methods, I seek to enter a space of immortality in certain time periods, to dance along with the chorus of the gods, explore the mysteries, and gain the reputation of a god. I have stowed away for myself many pieces of this school of thought and teachings from these books. I have trained myself in the tables and natures of the stars, a theoretical understanding of the signs, and how to make use of the astronomical tables of phases and appearances. In these teachings, I have combined all that I have acquired from previous collections.

In making a determination by degree, a combined viewing of the stars is required, and their signs, as well as exact degrees. In this way, any statement or logical analysis can be said with full truth. For often, I have had the experience of taking down the information in the chronograph of transits, which makes stars in other signs, and astronomical appearances, show up in others. This is especially true when they are in the beginning or end of the sign. Moreover, there is much stuttering in the stations of planets, including when they rise over the ridge at sunset. It is imperative to know accurately the nature and quality of the signs and degrees, and especially the ascendant, as this will make a solid determination. Therefore, let us make a beginning of a guiding principle. In scoping out the years laid down in the genesis, we take out as many portions of 12 as is possible. Then, the remaining number will be taken up in succession from a powerful star on a powerful place. In this giving over, we will know that a certain transfer happens in a certain year. The information laid down has been cut short, so the determination is complicated. All stars, the ascendant, Sun, and Moon transfer to each other and can be compared against one another.

Let us take an example, to create an extremely clear and distinct avenue inwards.

Sun and Mercury in Aquarius
Moon in Scorpio
Jupiter in Libra and Saturn in Cancer
Venus in Capricorn
Mars and Ascendant in Virgo

We can inquire into the 35th year. I subtract out 2 twelves, which is a total of 24.

11 Remains.

We calculate this 11 from the quantity of the star that will be overtaken first and the nature of its place. We now discover several things. Ascendant and Mars to Saturn in Cancer, then from the Moon to Mars (11), and from Venus to the Moon. All of the transfers are full of action and energy in the 35th year. The nature of each star, according to its power and potential to create a manifestable outcome, will yield a blessed fate or a foul one, which we will signify in these transfers; the nature of which has been outlined in the preceding logic.

It is necessary to judge together the entirety of all influences that will be involved in the transfers, whether exceedingly beneficial or injurious, and then to allot the wand of judgement in terms of those influences. If from equal places, the year will be judged as anomalous and spottled. Generally speaking, it will be necessary to cast out the yearly influences for the entire genesis from the Sun and

Moon. If they are fallen out in empty, fruitless places, the rulers of their signs will be taken alongside in the analysis. These three calculations have much power, whether the transfer is to occur in beneficial places or malefic ones, on pivots, in productive places, or out of the pivots. The other stars must be observed in the transfer. If malefics are thoroughly ruling the year, yet the three aphetic forces have the power of benefics, the year will be practical and significant, accompanied by doubts, fears, and troubles. If none of the stars transfer to a star but the distribution is carried into fruitless and empty places, it is necessary to pay attention to them; especially if certain stars will be trampling onto them by transit and will be received. It is necessary to cast out from the lots of fortune, spirit, eros, and *ananke*. It is from these influences, and their fitting, fruitful times, that exceptionally good energies, pathologies, and dangers will be absorbed.

It is most natural and quite necessary to cast out from the pivots. The same exact influences are often discovered in the generalities of life, the cosmic indications, and in the actual lives of humans and mankind. The year is analyzed by the eastern rising of the dog-star *Kunos* and the four ascensions of the pivots in terms of the *tetraeteridos*[8]. In addition, there will be subtle variances in the yearly influences, as seen in the schematic graph of the stars; various phases and appearances, and certain transits that will contribute to the creation of fitting and ripe times. Similarly the Sun makes four movements. A great one, a lesser one, and two mediocre ones. The circle keeps on course through these four turnings. There are four natural configurations of the Moon — new moon, cut in half, full moon, and a second cut in half phase. The same cosmic alignment is established in the earthly realm through the four elements and four winds. If all this is true, then we must utilize the four pivots in the genesis and release counting from them. This will provide a baseline for the yearly cycles and help synthesize these cycles with the stars in genesis. Each genesis has an exact unique nature in terms of the pivots and layout of zodiacal signs. One must also know the cosmic

---

[8] For more info on this, refer to the first book of the *Anthology*—Vettius Valens *Book 1.2, Chapter 4.*

conjunction cycles and eastern risings of the dog-star *Kunos*, as well as the hour, whether or not the tropics rise (solstice or equinox points), and the ruler of the eastern rising. In general terms, this ruler will be judged as the house-ruler of the year. There are also circular rulers of the places. Even further, there is a general ruler of each genesis (and anti-genesis), a yearly ruler (in terms of the circular cycles), and rulers of the new moon and full moon. We must synthesize the general ruler and cosmic ruler with the layout of the genesis, applying this information to each house and its properties. Moreover, we can notice whether the general rulers, cosmic rulers, and circular influences of genesis are harmonious in terms of their general properties. We can analyze influences coming to these rulers (and any eclipses), to see their effect on the nature of specific regions in the genesis; whether productive or not, via eastern risings and special appearances of stars. It is from the collection of these indications that one can make a determination of notable charts; those with leadership capacities and royal inclinations. Through this process, one can notice changes in praxis and reputation, as well as grand and wondrous outcomes, which will manifest in a customary manner. Some charts will indicate unsurpassable luck, while others are easy to conquer — weak and paltry in luck and life. Keeping all of this in mind, one must not appear to have too much to say, weaving a web from this school of thought. Instead, he should offer a steadfast delineation of the various influences, in order that the distribution is made with great precision, in both brilliant and mediocre nativities.

Also, when we inquire about life substance in terms of public reputation, social precedence, visionary capacities, fatherhood, and socializing with those of greater standing, it is customary to analyze the manifestation potential through the western quarter, where the Sun and stars set. We can begin the counting of years from this position. When we inquire into bodily dangers, pathologies, bloodshed, or motherhood, we can count from the Moon. For matters of praxis, livelihood, and artistic prowess, from the midheaven. When inquiring into good luck, and the gathering of resources, from the lot of fortune. For any affairs connected to death, great changes, or violence, from the setting place. When about foundations, acquisitions, things concealed, or topics related to death, from the place under the earth. When about a woman, inter-twinings, intimacy, and the form and image of wife, from Venus. For topics such as military affairs and politics, from Mars. When about the dismantling of business and assets, hidden pathologies, or inheritances from the father's lineage, from Saturn. When about nourishment, reputation, affiliations, collaborations, and acquisition of assets, from Jupiter. When about communications, servants, bodily matters, giving and receiving, or writings, from Mercury.

These lists offer up one image; a picture of what can occur during the transfer and reception of stars.

Let us discuss the situation of two, three, or more transfers and receptions occurring at the same time. In this case, we consider the potentials of each star, in reference to other stars present. Depending on the foundation chart set up at genesis, benefics and malefics will manifest contributing circumstances to the total life outcome. What manifests will depend on the configuration of the entire chart, each star's influence by angles cast, and all factors pertaining to its configuration. Something resembling this will indeed manifest, depending on each stars taking over for the time periods, and the one transferring over.

In order to see the most accurate and highly energized version of what is to manifest during a transfer, we should strive to establish concrete rules, recommendations, precepts, commands, and laws to guard this teaching and make it easy to apprehend. Earlier on, it was noted that we must observe whether transfers occur from places on certain pivots to others. We also might notice a transfer occurring from the place of beneficent spirit, into the lot of fortune (or another productive place). This will reveal a notable outcome of practical gifts and a good reputation. The transfers could also occur from places outside of pivots into pivots, or from the place of maleficent spirit into the region of good spirit. The most productive and energized regions are the ascendant, good spirit, good luck, and the lots of fortune, spirit, eros, & *ananke*[9]. The mediocre places are god, goddess, and the remaining two pivots. The other regions are considered midland to mean. Depending on what benefics or malefics witness them by angle, the potential of these regions can be utterly weak, or highly energized. In terms of bad luck from maleficent spirit, it seems better to possess a triangular configuration close to the midheaven.

Let us take the case of only one transfer found in genesis, as all stars have been produced in one sign. These stars will then transfer by sign. If a certain combination or aggregate is indicated in genesis, that mixture will participate in all things. If three or four stars are in discovered in one sign, and one or two in another, the first being earlier in a superior square by degree and allotted to the time periods (this is earlier because the most minimal period has taken up the degrees) and then one after another in succession, they will receive a similar thing from each successor.

---

[9] Find calculations for these lots in Vettius Valens *Anthology*, Book 2.1.2 @ **MoiraPress.com**.

Because the dissection of times is quite complicated, if one comes to it, he must not miss the mark entirely, utterly failing at the calculation. Since twelve of these transfers are signified, the energy is not the same for each manifestable outcome in succession. There are variances. Whenever we discover a transfer on a certain circle, from one or more influences, we must observe that year in the anti-genesis, and also in terms of the trampling along of stars, to see what kind of configurations it makes on the genesis. Also, if it makes a similar indication in the transfers and receptions, and whether it makes any similar appearance to the Sun. For if we discover such similarities, we would say that the outcomes to manifest will be steadfast. If there are unnatural combinations with dissimilar elements, manifestation will not quite be complete. There are general configurations and those by exact degree. For instance, if a person draws down the influence of a beautifully placed Saturn and Jupiter during a certain time, then another influence falls within the circle (also beaming down and informing the time), there could be an inheritance. The native could be highly energized by morbid topics and affairs of the dead. If Saturn or Jupiter are the ultimate ruler of the year in the second or third circle, but they are not rolling around beautifully, an inheritance will not occur. Instead, a legacy through the affairs of the dead, or the expectation for such things, will result. This could be the purchasing of properties and foundations, further acquisition of assets, fresh gains, etc. Similarly, other things will bring the steadfast manifestation of outcomes through the circle of twelve. Sooner or later, something will come to fruition; especially if there is an inner knowing about the life purpose and manifestation clearly exhibited in the stars.

Let us look at what things can occur in the first circle of genesis. For example, a marriage drawn down in year 34 (a synthesized judgement of manifestation potential per the Sun's position). Another circle speaks of intimacy, or marriage, and various other bits of information about when the wife will appear (things reach a peak point, etc.) and this will create a powerful vision on the subject.

Yet another will have gone to military service. The same transfer could bring advancement, changes, and great energy for a martial praxis. If the general foundation chart is successful, promotions will occur in ripe time periods, especially if the benefics are holding fast and supporting the equation. If a genesis is truly magnificent, he will participate in leadership positions, become an administrator, or begin a volunteer arrangement. It is necessary to be consistent with the genesis, in order to synthesize and harmonize the various aspects of potential outcomes to manifest.

Another individual might birth a child at a certain time. With the same transfer occurring at the acme of existence (the prime of life), they will furnish children or the purchasing of bodily things. Or, there will be physiological renewal in the offspring at certain degrees, or thoughts will center on foreign children. Another individual will come into authority and governance of the crowd. When the same chronograph occurs in a beautiful foundation of genesis, the native will take up magnificent, notable leadership roles. In mediocre charts, things such as these will be diverted and overturned. There will be fantasies of leadership or front seat positions and preferential treatment. Moreover, the individual will be judged and controlled. When the same transfer occurs from benefics and the angles they are making, he will escape controlling situations and avoid blame. If from malefics, he will survive the undertaking of highly corrupt work, accusations, blame, and grudges, or he will be dragged through something even worse.

The remaining will synthesize to manifest in the life, to the extent allowed by the transfer, and differences that exist through the general time graph, anti-genesis, transits, phases, and appearances of stars. Still, both schematic graphs could hold dissimilar elements. When the stars make a transit during a certain fitting and fruitful time on the places transferring in genesis, those receiving the transfer, or in the pivots, then they will join together in the allotment by their own unique natures to create a good manifestation or a foul one; an outcome that is highly energized or one withheld. Yet we make a secure judgement when a sympathetic configuration exists between a transiting star and the one making a transfer. Those transferring to those receiving have a similar configuration, for instance, in genesis. If the chronic indicators signify one thing but the yearly period and transits another, there will be a middle state between two extremes in the manifestation of telos. Generally speaking, any star in a transfer and reception that is in the setting region, placed down in a hindered, impractical way, and if a benefic is discovered, only *phantasias*[10] will be furnished. If the three apheses of Sun, Moon, and ascendant signify dissimilar elements, the year will be dappled and manifold; wrought with many colors. The transfer will often not occur in the same sect, yet if the general times are tremendous, and have laid down information indicating notable outcomes. From that fact, taking the beginning, it is necessary to advance through the yearly time period.

---

[10] ***Phantasia*** = appearance to the consciousness, imagination, vision (1916)

Certain authors have spoken in riddles about the compilation of treatises in the preceding school of thought. Yet those to come in the future will happen upon this collection, powerfully made and arranged by myself, and will be wooed from the beginning. No one has investigated this new method yet. Necessarily, we must point out the hooks. Meaning, the things that are to occur at the transfer, according to a form and image of a fully expressed outcome. In this way, we can manifest the most wondrous and energized outcome possible. If one is to approach future predictions, speaking in a discreet and sober manner, and point out places in which transfers will occur, they offer a synthesized viewing of the energies of a star and its sign, and continue on with great precision.

ιβ; On the Names and Natures
of the Twelve Places

Let's begin from ascendant.

1. Helm of life, body, breathe.

2. Livelihood. "Gate of Hades." A shaded region, giving and receiving in the corporate marketplace. Interminglings with women, reconciliation with praxis, help from affairs of the dead, a place of disposition of property by will.

3. Brothers, friendliness with kin, abundance through foreign royalty, giving the heart to a slave.

4. Reputation of children, marriage partners as a private interest, the visage of elders, political praxis, property, houses, returning to solitude, changes in location, dangers of death, constraint through the mysteries.

5. The place of children, a friendliness to the freedom of bodily expression among common people, a drawing out of a plethora of good things and well crafted works.

6. Sickness of slaves, enmity, pathologies, weakness.

7. Marriage, lucky occurrences, intertwining with the wife, affiliations, foreignness.

8. Death, inasmuch as there is aid through morbid matters, an idle place, weak in righteousness.

9. Friendliness to life abroad, aid in foreign countries, help from a god, power of royalty, utilization of astronomical laws, appearance of gods, prophetic gifts, powers of divination, taking part in mystical and hidden affairs.

10. Reputation as praxis, advancement, success, prosperity of children and the woman. A transition of practical affairs, becoming commonly known.

11. Affiliations, hopes, gifts, children, total freedom through bodily affairs.

12. Foreign enmity, enslavement, illness, danger, tests and trials, pathologies of weakness, death.

Each region signifies its own manifestations and shares its operation with the region opposed to it. When a transfer occurs in the year, observe the nature of the regions where the transfer happens. In which of the preceding places is the receiving star? The specific manifestation will become clear by the nature of house and sign, and the outcomes of that place. In terms of the star handing over, it will have its own potential manifestations. We set up the distribution in terms of telos. For instance, if Saturn or Mars is on the ascendant, making a transfer, or receiving the other, we would say (in that year) there will be bodily distress, danger, or bloodshed. If in the seventh sign from the ascendant, the native could be misled by women, there could be danger through a woman, or great tumult in marriage. If the transfer occurs in the ninth place from the ascendant, there will be precarious situations foreign in nature, altercations in a foreign country, abandonment by foreigners, etc. In the twelfth region, grief through slaves, stand-offs, and enemies. Each region also has a certain magnitude of manifestation potential. A star will allow for a certain action, regarding the things condoned by that region.

If the benefics are in these places, a good thing will be signified. Help through good reputation, for instance, or a passion for purchasing foreign items. Decisions will occur during the taking over of a star, in terms of what is on or witnessing its place. From the nature of the star handing over and also the one receiving it, and their regions, an image of manifestable outcomes will develop from these factors. The disembarking will be judged in terms of the pragmatic affairs.

Look to the ruler of the places transferring and receiving to see the sort of signs in which the formation occurs. This star will provide action and operation towards the manifestation of that image and form. The second sign from the ascendant and the eighth, are idle; judged to be deadly. When a transfer and reception occurs in these regions, help and aid will be motivated through matters of the dead, especially when benefics are on or witnessing them. In this case, help will come from great individuals. If malefics, the judgement will be disputable because of the reception. The year will bring danger, mischief, and impracticality. This is the case when only malefics are in these places. Sun, Moon, or Mercury will bring bloodthirsty complaints, danger, and fighting. If Venus is on or witnessing one of these places, there will be trouble from drugs, plotting, scheming, suspicion, and resentment. These places also indicate death during the transfer of Saturn, inheritance with the transfer to Jupiter, and a life that gets help from matters of the dead. If the same transfer runs together in the first chronograph, inheritance will be inalterable. There can be great help, depending on the foundation of genesis. If distribution occurs in the gates of Hades and at the same time, and Saturn hands over to the house of Jupiter, there will be inheritance. This transfer, on its own, brings help from affairs of the dead. Suppose Saturn and Jupiter are handing over and receiving in the same sign. When the transfer occurs from the region of good spirit (11th House), good luck (5th House), or the lot, and benefics are on these places, there will be inheritance, gifts, and foreknowledge of very good news. If somehow a place of death makes a transfer to a cadent region, or a cadent region to a place of death, the native will hear of death from a foreign source. The four cadent regions signify places of foreigners and slavery. Moreover, Gemini and Sagittarius in general, for the entire chart, because of their cosmic effect, signify regions that speak to slavery. A Cancer ascendant sets down the topic of slavery in these places. If another sign has the topic of slavery,, and malefics are found in these places, upheaval will occur from slaves. Unrighteousness will manifest through punishments, death, or running away, especially if Saturn comes up to these places. If benefics are on them, a kind disposition and assistance will be given from these things. They will have good action and operation in these places, restoring and renewing certain aspects of life, in terms of the fates of children. Let the same thing be known for the remaining cadent regions.

ιγ; On the Transfer from a High Place into a High Place

Esteemed and helpful transfers occur from one high place into another, especially when benefics are on or bearing witness and rulers are in their own places. Moreover, when transfers occur from stars in their own houses into their exaltations, or from exaltations into houses of their rulership, on places that create highly energized outcomes, these transfers will signify glorious manifestations. A transfer will be more mediocre when occurring from a weak and fallen place, into another weak place; resulting in anomalous outcomes. Saturn or Mars configured by house from their own places or exaltations, or productive regions, giving over and receiving, will bring fruition to great mixings of action and high esteem. When inheritance comes from Saturn, there will be acquisition of land, foundations that produce revenue, the ability to manage such resources, the taking up of mysteries, and an uprightness over ancient affairs. From Mars, authority and leadership. We must also observe the luminaries by house (Sun and Moon), to see if they have been configured through great manifestations, bringing help and aid to life's outcomes. When far away from benefics, in opposition or configured in some alien way (with Mercury intermingling), allegations and oppositions will occur, as well as great danger leading to plots, schemes, uproar, and destruction. On exaltations of others, or making a transfer and reception in houses not their own, there will be wounds and bloodshed, as the native is thrown from high places and four footed animals. Upheaval will come through dangerous illness, inflammation, and tumult through shipwreck. In the spirit of helping the genesis, the stars can be drawn down to aid life and reputation.

We must look to see if the chart is classified as daytime or nighttime and notice the configuration of other parts. Notice those highly charged up with action for a good thing, and other potentials available in the remaining stars. By transfer of house rulerships and things set down in the tramping along of the great benefics. If another, they will hinder and check the reputation and bring helpful things. When malefics will have been named according to this, they are able to diminish the life force. There will be good operation and action in terms of the remaining things. Since Jupiter and Venus are taking over in the transmission and trampling along in the setting region, they are fallen aside; not in their own houses. In this configuration, they will manifest troublesome times, involving disquiet, stressful work, and extraordinary hopes and expectations about what one will do. Help and aid can also be diminished, which will lead to damages and penalties during such times. This will test the spirit in the accomplishing of evil things.

ιδ; On Appearances of the Stars.
And the Trampling Along of Transits.

Generally speaking, it is required to observe all stars. When a star is rising in the east, handing over or receiving a transfer, ruling the year and general time, trampling along in productive places, creating a beautiful rise above the eastern horizon, practical affairs will manifest fully and plainly. The power of the stars will rouse the native, stirring him into a particular nature, unique to each star, and its essence. Manifestations will follow. Depending on the qualities and powers governing the unique manifestation potentials in natal chart, and the indications of year and sign, there will be a divine, supernatural operation behind the makings of the specific manifestation at hand. If retrograde, then at the first station, the expectations for productivity will come to fruition through help, aid, and undertaking anything that delays the process. Moreover, there will be great weakness in the tips of the nails and a hindering through this, the foreshowing offering only visions and hopes. If at the second station, postponements will be removed and certain praxes will be reestablished. There will be good health and a straightforward quality to the livelihood. If stars are carried to the setting place, they can produce interruptions, grief, etc., while also providing accomplishments. They can bring bodily danger, weakness, and toil in hidden places. The setting configuration often foreshows high hopes, good reputation, and offerings to a god. When a malefic is manifesting through the natal chart (has the year, etc.), and a malefic is trampling along by transit and walks into it, the malefic force will increase. If a benefic, there will be comfort and aid. Imagine a similar situation, but benefic. By elimination, in terms of the entire genesis, when Jupiter's region is active by the trampling along, or the places square or opposite to it, and it has the time period, the native will fare beautifully in productive places, manifesting a good reputation and great, well-made works, especially when Jupiter is rising in the east. The factors seeming to ultimately rule the time period will grow stronger. When the star trampling across the regions of a malefic is weak, there will be good energy and reputation, accompanied by elevated overbids. If it happens to be east rising, the native will be comforted and helped within due limits.

ιε; On the Third and Ninth Regions from the Ascendant.

When a handing over and receiving occurs in the third or ninth place from ascendant, and benefics are in these places, a good thing will manifest through foreignness. Or, there will be advancement of the praxis through foreign people, commendations, etc. If the region happens to be inhabited by a mutable sign, help will come often, or many things will occur in foreign lands. Some stars are quite useful in these places — for godly things, future prognostications, atonements to a god, prayer, and offerings in a temple. Some configurations suggest weak intuition because of a god, control, blame, pathologies, danger, or escaping from a god and rejoicing in this escape. Yet in a glorious foundation, planetary energies will combine in certain time periods. Gifts will be accepted from royalty via practicality. And, the native will hold the beliefs and abundance of a leader. Things set down will bring about a notable reputation, becoming simultaneously responsible for the unravelling of royal luck. Some will prepare a ship or holy place for royalty. Others take up prophetic sayings, and in doing so, create an everlasting remembrance. Malefics on (or witnessing) these places, will bring about disparaging remarks in foreign countries, punishment, and encounters with needy people; preventing amends in the foreign country. There will be entrapments and danger through wandering. Those feeling a vengeful temper from a god will continue onward with manifestation, dissatisfied with their fates of allotment. Some deny the goddess during time periods. Others feel divine awe and fear, eating unlawful meats. They may come into foreknowledge, offer oracles, exercise powers of divination, and take up these studies in a maniacal, frantic, or mad way. Those in a greater position will have set down a good reputation from foreignness. There could be notorious scandals through foreign places. A rising up in the crowd and city affairs, from which the native will not rejoice due to dangerous circumstances; enveloped in a cloud of lingering hatred and abandonment. This kind of thing could surround the native with accusations among scary, royal people; bringing down the reputation, yet preserving the life and livelihood.

ις; On Anomalies in Natal Charts.

Before all else, we must examine the foundational arrangement of the entire birth chart at genesis. We use this information to make certain determinations. It is crucial to know the nature of the stars and signs and how they fit together. With a thorough analysis, we can make sure to not declare the same manifestation as "mediocre or honorable," and notice the existence of subtle variations. Each star and sign has an average nature, able to bring about work well done or grim things (depending on the presentation), with high esteem or a harsh tone. We can certainly say that the natal chart, set down at birth, can be responsible for gloriously blessed or brutally horrible things.

When we discover a significant, brilliant, foundation natal chart — thoroughly guarded by aspects from benefics in certain times — which then give over to times held by malefics, also affected by the trampling of stars, released in pivots or productive places, we can say that nothing is out of place. There will be inheritances, but the native will be entirely unorganized in managing the house and affairs. And he will be notorious for these faults. There will be fearful situations, uproars, etc. If somehow the Sun, new moon, or full moon regions are maltreated, unlawful and violent situations will bring upheaval. The native will survive danger and become well known for this. He could rise up in political affairs, in the midst of great hatred, agitatedly continuing onward, rejoicing nonetheless. A synthesized judgement of factors is crucial. Are benefics present or witnessing? In what ways can the native run alongside all foretold forces, especially anything that might bring him down or create dishonor?

If only the Moon or ascendant is maltreated, bodily irritations and invisible, precarious illnesses will arise. The reputation will be grievous from the beginning because of things acquired. If the foundation of genesis is somehow impractical, found passing through its own unique manner of livelihood, (not in the transfer of times, nor in things set out to occur in the manifesto-graph through trampling alongs, etc.), we must say that the practical affairs are complex, spotted, paradoxical, and contrary to expectation.

Nor will this create new forms of praxis, or changes in praxis. There will be little true and complete happiness *(eudaimonia)*. The malefics trampling through productive places, damaging things greatly. The benefics do not help the mediocre state of things because of the existence of a general preconceived notion, which we are not able to exchange in the portion. Many charts are brought down from great luck, honor, etc., into a lower or weaker state. Others have an arrangement that changes from mediocre luck, to dishonor through the family, to a state of blessed and happy spirit, surrounded by prominence. When a genesis is carried into a high place (as discovered from generalities of sect) into beneficial times of the chronograph (by part, when benefics are holding the time period, signifying a brilliant quality, providing help and advancement), closely attend to these things. The periods held by malefics have an elevated state to them, causing tumult through bodily nuisances; yet the foundation persists, not to be overthrown. If somehow the genesis is carried into a lower or weaker state (as indicated by the generalities of foundation), and benefics take over the yearly periods (weak stars trampling along in transits), the native will come into a state of good energy, yet yield to malefics, damaging the chart greatly. In this way, benefics do not always have a benefic function, nor do the malefics always hold a malefic function, as it depends on the general structure of the foundation, in terms of the parts of the chronograph that benefics are alternating crosswise.

We can lay out the arrangement of practical gifts for each genesis, whether Mercury, Mars, Venus, or Saturn is holding the action; or from the Sun, Moon, and Jupiter, in the case that foundation is proven reputable. In these transfers, each star is beautifully configured. Or in its approach, as it tramples along in a transit, the year will bring help and honor in any practical affairs the native occupies. For instance, Saturn coming to the place of the Sun or Moon, will indicate things from each of their particular natures, depending on the placement, damaging those things greatly. Similarly, if the year is on Saturn or has fallen into it (in the genesis and also where it is trampling along), we can speak about the things involved in its manifestable outcomes.

The remaining stars, Sun, and Moon, in busy places, and the time rulers are set down full of action, yet opposed, this will bring tumult. In terms of the entire nativity, if some piece of information is laid down about the year from Sun, Moon, and ascendant, good and bad things could be indistinguishable. For instance, if things are fallen out via Venus or Jupiter, in productive places, this is good. If the places have been maltreated by Saturn or Mars, this is paltry. If the transfer comes to both, clearly indicated by the stars and their places, all of these things will occur in this year. If three calculations indicate dissimilar elements, the year will be anomalous and inconsistent. It is better when the transfer occurs from malefic to benefic regions, than benefic to malefic ones. If a star transfers to another star, and they are in one sign (the one who governs the house in a productive place), the time will manifest productively.

The following logic seems most natural. When something is signified from each place, and the aphesis of years comes there, these things will occur. For instance, when we inquire about praxis from the midheaven and the place speaking to marriage, this could indicate women and slavery. If we discover benefics in places where the counting stops (present or witnessing), and the sign is also productive, we can see straightforward affairs, help, and disembarking on plans close to one's heart and mind. Look at the entire picture in a synthesized way, house ruler of house ruler, etc., to see the nature of the sign in which a star falls, and how it has been configured. If a ruler is well placed, but there is an incongruity of position with some mean thing, aid will come at certain times, helping to accomplish hopes and dreams. Some will accept beliefs and gifts from greater, kingly types. This is the case when combining the general times of Sun and Moon, with a judgement of benefics. The finer divisions also look beautiful. In general, this is very true in a genesis where Jupiter is in a superior square to Saturn; or a conjunction, square, triangle, opposition, etc. If Mars is found in a triangle or square to it, in the region that sits right above setting, and Jupiter is in the place under earth, the gifts and aid will be greater. Supplying gifts to others, they enjoy a good reputation among the populace, becoming consumed by the crowd. If found not configured under Saturn, Mars, or Mercury in the genesis, and witnessed instead by Jupiter and Venus, the native will come to love a good reputation, increased *euphemia*[11], participation, and honors. If gazed upon by Mars, he will change his mind, complain, cause trouble, chat endlessly about scandals, and dissolve inward. If by Saturn, the native will survive dangerous situations and blame, sparingly and cautiously. If by benefics, both will occur together.

Every angle of a star can be powerful, except the square and diameter. This technique uses those in signs of the same ascensional times. When the transmission occurs in Taurus and Virgo, it indicates manifestable outcomes with an instability from these places, elevated through the legal process, and all it entails. In Sagittarius and Capricorn, things are riddling and dark. Penalties can occur, as these signs are ineffectual, not manifesting outcomes. It is most

---

[11] **Euphemia** = words of good omen, abstinence from inauspicious language, religious silence, a favorable name for something, euphemism (a good name for a bad thing (736)

natural to make the distribution, not only scoping out the genesis in terms of planetary transfers, but also the *katarchic charts*[12], knowing the hour and arrangement of constellations, utilizing the same methods in the election as are used in a genesis. When Saturn and Mars hold logic over the Sun, Moon, and ascendant, in terms of oppositional aspects, superior squares, and other configurations, there is the potential for meanness. If somehow the genesis does not yet indicate child rearing, separate out manifestable outcomes by potential. For instance, the beginning of praxis will be discovered by the transfer of stars, as they bring manifestable outcomes to father and mother. In terms of rulership, the one born will be overtaken until the acme of existence, at which point the native will take over the course of significations. Yet there is only the power to make way for that which is allotted, so we might leave behind a legacy of gifts, naming two things that occur simultaneously. For instance, a slackened

---

[12] ***katarchic charts*** = beginning, forecast of an undertaking or voyage, primacy, starting point (910).

*Modern day equivalent would be the *electional chart*.

condition with low tension of the blood vessels, and flowers and blooms bursting forth at the same time (breaking out, ulcers, etc). In this way, there will be a synthesis of manifestations that seem paradoxical, those contrary to expectation. Yet this will occur in a manner customary to such indications, where things will clearly be indicated beforehand, by the general combined mixing and judgement of stars. It is necessary, depending on the prime years of life, and according to the years of certain places and their spheres of command, to combine and harmonize various manifestations, according to the significations of the times. For it is in this way that the pragmatic tendencies can be determined in a straightforward manner, involving no deceit. In terms of the twofold nature of nativities, it is necessary per the topic of siblings, the man or woman, kin, or other loved ones, to look to the house arrangement of genesis. Here we are observing evidence of a certain outcome according to a specific time cast in the chart. It is said that things will come together sooner or later, distributed in the manner of another part (a second portion). For instance, if some influence is carried to a place which indicates help from matters of the dead, and this is the prognostication, yet there is another thing indicated by the general allotment (from which there will be help in manifesting the expectations of the aforementioned thing), the help will not occur in these time periods, but in periods expected depending on what has been inherited in the allotment. From the midheaven, when there is an outcome being manifested, often the manifestation will come about quickly. And yet, in another time period, this same signature might be responsible for life abroad, judgement, accusations, and other such blameworthy things. Let it be know that a similar thing will be true about the reputation, gifts, purchasing, praxis, fellowship, wedlock, foreignness, and any other combined manifestations in the life.

In this custom of apprehending life manifestations before they come to pass, any slowness or sluggishness in making things happen can come through sympathies and antipathies in the natal chart. Just as is written at length and in detail about the nature, in the table of calculations, per the rising up of stars, and the concurrent potentials for manifestable outcomes. Unexpectedly, the native will be carried into a thing they were not aware of, stretched out and increased in intensity, being held fast by the fates of necessity. This will go on until the native has acquired a harmonized version of the pragmatic affairs.

It is necessary to set out examples of cosmic alignments, so we can come to know the process of synthesis. The Sun does not always make the same change to the airs when it hits the degrees of the solstices and equinoxes. But when a certain cosmic position of the heavens (taken beforehand) leads to a good temperature, the wintery turns will be calm, fine, clear, mild, and gracious. Later, there will be storms, copious amounts of driving rain, and powerful winds. We have prepared and furnished a suspenseful and decisive moment. The Moon is not strong enough, by what is expected based on its appearances, to bring together heavy rains through bondage of the airs. It might have been stormy beforehand. This previous nature must be considered (which is to blame for the storm), and added to the expectations of what might occur.

The mixture may not have occurred at fitting times. The wintery configurations were also not entirely indicated, as in the same appearance, calm and gracious airs were set down. A passing from hand to hand is also indicated, and an interchange that occurs at the loosening of the bonds. The airs will have transformed to a wintery state. Moreover, the remaining significant appearances of stars and their settings will not occur according to these influences. Instead, they will make a preconceived notion of appearances that will occur later, and in this way are not entirely indicative. Things come together by the inter-lacings of eastern risings throughout the year; new moons, full moons, eclipses, appearances during the four-year terms, etc. Also, from a generic description of house rulers around the circle, and inter-lacings per the trampling of the stars during transits, as well as subsequent extractions of manifestations during fitting time periods.

ιζ; **On the Transfer of Stars, Manifestable Outcomes, and the Ascendant**

We shall now set up the transfers of the stars.

The Sun giving over to Saturn manifests a year oppressed by toil. There is an impracticality as this transfer signifies oppositions, hatred, illogical situations from those having the upper hand, meanness from older people, illness through rising up in rank, anomalies in eyesight, livelihood, movements, fearful situations with superiors, increased burdens, and death (or a similar situation) related to the father. If the stars have fallen in a mean way, manifestations will bring blame and oppression.

The Sun transferring to Jupiter indicates a brilliant year, a good reputation for the father, collaborations with those above, prosperity, gifts, significant and notable praxis, beginnings, and the conception of children. This transfer brings marriage to the unmarried, effectiveness in accomplishing things, positivity, directness, and good hopes.

The Sun to Mars indicates a precarious and sickly year, danger to the father, and other things characterized by the transfer. There will be upheaval to the practical affairs through inquiry and examination, straightforward accomplishment of the practical affairs, payments, untimely punishments, enmity from those with a greater social visage, the father being forced into submissive roles, mean cuts, bloodshed, the rising of blood, hard work in places of leadership, darkness, grudges, responsibilities, and threats.

The Sun to Venus indicates a good time. One that brings love. There will be introductions, gifts, friendliness all around, enjoyment through intimacy, marriage, children, and cosmic, bodily purchases. For those in dignified leadership positions there will be notable gifts, great hopes over the practical affairs, and deliverance from all blame.

The Sun to Mercury is good, practical, profitable and advantageous for fellowship. There will be good works accomplished in the face of submissive circumstances, and effectiveness in giving and receiving. If somehow looked upon by malefics, this will lead to lawsuits, upheaval, rejoicing in making money, fear of things written, thinking ill of slaves and loved ones, untimely payments, and penalties.

The Sun to Moon is practical and philanthropic, manifesting acquisition of resources, help from men and women, coming together through marriage, cooperation, significant offspring, resources from foreign countries, prosperity and health through said foreignness, and gifts.

The Sun giving over to itself during finer allotments, configured well, will manifest a brilliant and significant time for practical affairs; connections with prominent, magnificent individuals, and help from unexpected sources. If the Sun is with benefics, or witnessed by them, this will lead to aid through a greater reputation. Nocturnally this is worse, manifesting upheaval, hatred, judgements, grudges, and blame. If the Sun falls together with a malefic, or one is witnessing the Sun, the livelihood will diminish and the reputation will be tarnished; life will be precarious and involve foreignness, hatred of the father, danger, or tumultuous practical affairs.

It necessary to observe the nature of the stars in the schematic graph. In terms of house placement and class (each star configured well in the foundation of genesis), the power and potential for full manifestation of life the path and purpose will exist within. The aspects witnessing the remaining parts of the chart, and the trampling along of transits, have great potential for destruction, or to intensify and prolong a bad thing. They can also help, or create a certain reputation. It is better when they are in productive signs, rising in the east. If they happen to be under the setting point, malefic forces fallen aside, not in fitting house placements, the native can set out an offering to a god on the table, in times of opposition.

ιη; The Yearly Distribution of the Moon

The Moon to itself imparts unpleasantness. It leads to hatred and unrighteousness from those with a better reputation, affects worthiness of livelihood, and bring confrontations from women. If a malefic is viewing it, bodily weakness, and unexpected danger result. Observe, in this time, what is on the Moon's sign, making sure a malefic won't create some mean manifestation as it tramples along. If a benefic is present, the responsibilities will release, except with foreign affairs and changes in location. When in impassable places, business will be straightforward; the manifestations paltry and ordinary.

Moon to Sun imparts emptiness to the livelihood and large payments; especially if looked at by a malefic star, hindering the praxis by foreshadowing empty hopes, stand-offs, domestic upheaval, anarchy, entanglements with females, and marriage. For those in good standing, this transfer will bring a good reputation to the praxis, full payments in the marketplace, straightforward pragmatic affairs, advancement, gifts, and work well done.

The Moon to Saturn imparts a complicated year, bringing weakness and death to the mother. If going around, hatred and anarchy will infiltrate the pragmatic affairs leading to changes in location, cooling of the praxis, bodily dangers, the hiding of hard work, or sensations in the *aistheterion*[13]. A saltiness will arise through the diminishing. When rising in the east, the time will be less bad, except for a little mischief and distress.

Moon to Jupiter indicates a good and practical time, acquisition of resources, communication with great people, help in reputation, beginnings from females, and gifts. Marriage will come to the unmarried, intimacy with grow with children and loved ones, and increased livelihood to the mother. For those who have a good reputation and are straightforward in pragmatic affairs, everything will come together to manifest the hopes, fears, expectations, etc.

---

[13] ***Aistheterion*** = "Soul-Senses-Machine."

Literally, the place that houses the senses. Was thought to exist in the head, eyes, and down the body. For more on this concept, see Porphyry's *Ensoulment* @ MoiraPress.com

The Moon handing over to Mars leads to a harsh year, especially when carried up in the east during the day. This transfer will manifest danger, weakness, bloodshed, falls, fires, extra payments, penalties, instability at home with females, death, separations, hatred, judgements in unions, and rebellion among the masses. If the Moon had been carried under the setting point, most especially at night, when the time periods are on this region, things would be simple and ordinary. The manifestation of what is cast will not be easy and upright, but will come alongside fearful situations, and the execution of painful tasks.

The Moon to Venus indicates a shrewd, intelligent, and effective time, good reputation, unions, sympathies from men and women, and marriage. If somehow these stars are in houses alien to their nature (or looked upon by malefics), the time will be unpleasant, including jealousy, money spent on the face of a woman, and breaches of faith. In general, this exact transfer always leads to instability, unions, jealous anger, enmity towards kin, those in the home, and friendly seeming people.

The Moon to Mercury is practical and easily affected. There will be introductions to those with a feminine visage, especially when configured by benefics. If with malefics, there will be judgments and upheaval, yet rejoicing in survival, money, writing, and counting; though a great struggle will remain. If Mercury is in its own place, the native will be surrounded. If out of place, judgements and sentencing will occur, creating huge payments.

ιθ; The Yearly Distribution of Ascendant

The ascendant transferring to a malefic brings a mean time. Especially with Saturn at night and Mars during the day. This transfer leads to bodily danger, anomalous livelihood, fear, upheaval, falls, and illness.

Ascendant to Jupiter indicates a brilliant time, resources, good reputation, etc. This is a truly significant arrangement. There will be help and advancement through great people. In this time, some put an end to dangerous, blame-worthy situations. They become easily consoled, setting things back in order, trying their hand at freedom.

Ascendant to Venus indicates a wonderful time to become involved in aphrodisial affairs, new unions, intertwining with women in the marketplace, general mirth and merriment, and the deliverance from mean things.

Ascendant to Sun brings great sympathy from great individuals and superiors. Resources will be acquired. For those who already have a great reputation, the year will bring success, advancement, and promotions.

Ascendant to Moon indicates a practical change, help from women, collaborations that renew the praxis, and effectiveness in foreign places. When benefics are witnessing, expect prosperity in a foreign country. The gaze of malefics will bring opposition, in terms of the regions stars are on, and upheaval.

Ascendant to Mercury is practical, advantageous, and effective. If harmed by malefics, the native will go through the judicial process and receive fines.

Ultimately, stars giving over to ascendant bring similar outcomes. Depending of course on the layout of houses, how the arrangement interacts with each star (point), and how they interact with each other. Life outcomes can be judged as manifesting a blessed thing, or an ordinary one.

κ; The Yearly Distribution of Saturn.

Saturn giving over to itself signifies idle portions of time and annoyances. There will be enmity from great and older people, dishonor, interruptions to what is cast, and an instability towards the praxis. If Saturn is observed by Mercury or Mars, blackmail (through writing), judgement, dismantling through ancient matters, affairs of the dead, or bad work by slaves will result; or the native will persevere despite wrath from a god. He will be kind, slow, and sluggish, yet effective at certain things.

Saturn giving over to Sun will bring danger or death to the father (if there is already some weakness present in him), a prominent year through enmity, punishment, trials in the *aistheterion*, hard work, relapse of pathologies, or meanness of spirit at home and towards loved ones. If the days have been configured well, there will be hindrances bringing full payment and help from the dead or dying.

Saturn to the Moon brings danger to the mother; if not the mother, then through a female character. There will be hatred, harm through separations, mean actions, upheaval of business affairs, instability in movement, bodily weakness, chronic pathology of the senses through the sinew and nerves, distress within, injections, darkness, and various unexpected pathologies.

Saturn to Mars imparts a year of meanness and danger. There will be weakness, plots, disturbances, death, upheaval under his own, judgements, remaining alive through loved ones, not enjoying things at home, anarchy, accusations, fear towards larger individuals, hatred of the father, death, precariousness, impracticality through foreign relations, and people who seem older or more mature. If Saturn and Mars are poorly placed, manifestations can include shipwreck, pathologies, and illness. If well placed in productive signs or in configurations or witnessed by benefics, there will be great responsibilities, cast out to the wind.

Saturn to Jupiter indicates a beautiful and practical time. There will be legacies and inheritance, help from elders and dead people, the governing of foundations and resources, acquisition from watery sources (the native might become a shipowner, do purchasing on a ship, rebuild a ship), a carrying down of something ancient, and a straightforward, cosmic communion infiltrating the livelihood and practical affairs. If there is an aspect from Mars or Mercury, he will survive judgements, litigation, and ill-timed payments.

Saturn to Venus will create separations with women, or general injustice from females. Certain authors see death, instability, and the sharing of lives through intertwinements. They mention plots and schemes, experimentation with drugs and pharmaceuticals, surviving in the crowd, weakness, dampness, chills, the impact of being surrounded by flow, oppositional vibes, judgements, and the praxis becoming commonly known among the public. If the chart is of a woman, she will be dragged through anguish, especially if with child in the womb. There will be instability with friends over a man.

Saturn to Mercury brings ancient affairs, controversy over the mysteries, money, calculations, giving and receiving, interruption in accomplishing tasks, betrayal through damage, fines, and hatred. These natives witness the death of their own, get involved with multiple stories, and are surrounded by work in these times. They also make pledges, acquire debts, and get in trouble because of writings; depending on the schematic graph of horoscope and whether stars are in homey regions or places foreign to them. When square or opposite, they become quite mean, bringing life down, fear and upheaval through the subject of death.

κα; The Yearly Distribution of Jupiter

Jupiter handing over to itself imparts a good, practical time, help from friends, gifts, straight-forward belief in business, inheritance, communing with great individuals, and the conception of children. If viewed by Mars, anomalous and untimely payments will result.

Jupiter to the Sun imparts brilliance and a time of acquiring resources. It leads to beginnings among those with high social standing, annoyances over health and prosperity, advancements, honor, being deemed very worthy, chaplets of leadership, the office of a general, and significations of luck through authority positions. The exact manifestation depends on the arrangement of foundation and layout of stars among the houses. The praxis will be mediocre. Mean situations end. Freedom comes through commendations. There will be help from this change in astral weathers, sympathy among loved ones, the creation of children, and fresh gains in bodily matters, especially when well configured during the daytime.

Jupiter to Saturn creates movement towards prominence, full payments, disobedience at home, changes in certain things, death, location, business, instability among the populace, hatred among loved ones, ineffectiveness in accomplishing things, a straightforward approach to promotion, the learning of manners, increased demands, and stress.

Jupiter to Mars creates harmful, disturbing years, conflicts with superiors, false accusations, moral condemnation, abandonment of things acquired, dangerous situations involving foreignness, illness, precariousness among their own, anomalies around death that affect livelihood, and full payments. If the genesis is political or militant in nature, when well configured, collaborations and promotions that come along with payments and gifts, are overshadowed; and enduring suspicion through fearful situations.

Jupiter to Venus leads to acquisition of resources, involvement with aphrodisial affairs, unions, and gifts; either from women or through socializing with women. To the unmarried, it brings friendliness and diversion through beautiful entanglements. To those who have already joined in marriage, it brings conception and children. In notable charts, it offers honor (signified through wreaths, chaplets, etc.), significant rank through leadership, political involvement, gifts among the masses, and great promotions. This time can also manifest positions of authority or bodily and cosmic resources.

Jupiter to Mercury can bring a reasonable, advantageous unravelling of the practical affairs, leading to aid through logic, reckoning, and writing. It draws down fellowship, friendly associations with the greats, gifts, drawings, delineations, helpful situations from things entrusted to the native, and inventions. From this transfer, when a love of beauty is set down in the foundation, there will be purchasing of bodily items. Some will push forward if beautifully placed. In general, there will be false accusations and slander among the crowd, disquiet, and survival through scandal; especially when stars are poorly configured, opposed, conjunct, or squared by malefics. Natives will endure through mental struggles, battles, etc., continuing onward through frightful experiences.

Jupiter to the Moon provides an effective year, a time of acquiring resources from women, collaborations with greater characters, helpful gifts, leadership positions, authority, release from danger, cosmic, bodily acquisitions, conception, children, the gifts of intertwining with women, drawings, delineations, and good energy from the mother. If the schema is well configured, these natives can govern anything entrusted to them. Deposits, things stored in a vault, etc., will manifest. The stars also bring wealth through invention, being thankful to a god for a mean thing, and release from enslaving situations.

κβ; The Yearly Distributions of Mars

Mars handing over to itself imparts nausea in the daytime and upheaval. It leads to hatred, harm, threats over affairs of the populace, and being consumed through the democratic process. Some undergo abuse and become authority figures, take on the office of a general, etc. This is not negative in a night chart and creates an upright quality. More notably when set down in productive signs, coming together into a martial praxis, such as political or military affairs.

The transfer of Mars to the Sun brings danger to the father; if not to the father himself, to a father figure. It also manifests conflict with superiors, separation from loved ones, sickness, precariousness, hard work in the *aistheterion*, danger, bloodshed from fire, and falls from high places and four footed animals. It can lead to cuts, jealous collapse, controversy, and fearful situations in foreign lands. If somehow in productive signs, witnessed by benefics, help will come to both praxis and reputation through commendations by superiors. The advancement will be accompanied by fearful situations, confusion, plots, malice, and hindering of the business affairs.

Mars to the Moon is perilous. This transfer is dangerous, unstable, oppressive, involves fear and lawsuits, precariousness through foreign affairs, increased burdens through foreigners, abusive threats, danger from the mother, fights with a female character, separations, uproars in the crowd or the city, weakness, bloodshed, falls into pathology, survival through fire, danger, and shipwreck. More often in a day chart (the Moon increasing in light and poorly fallen), things will be worse. The native will walk away from things written prior, be overshadowed through trauma, break limbs, have illness to the eyes, and eyestrain. If witnessed by benefics in productive places, the manifestation will be a fearful praxis that brings advancements. In the charts of females, blood will bring bodily danger, deterioration, the cutting of a fetus due to natural causes, and extremely hard work in certain places.

Mars to Saturn brings a mean and disorderly year, lawsuits, threats, punishment, rejection, breaches of faith, danger and death to his own, violent ill will, tumultuous productivity surrounded by foreignness, grievous situations from pirate vessels and burglars, weak blood flow, unexpected danger, rising up through hatred, lawsuits, grievances from slavery, pledges, oppression, and the drawing out of painful or fearful apologies. Unless in fitting sign-house placements or witnessed by benefics, the native will take up the responsibilities in a way as to just scratch the surface.

Mars to Jupiter indicates a beautiful, practical year, leading to straightforwardness, help from great individuals, collaborations, hope for good things, and things synthesizing to fully manifest expectations and hopes for the future. This transfer has the logic of military affairs. For a chart that is naturally involved with the military, there will be promotions. Those in a greater status will come into leadership roles, gaining a significant and notable reputation. On a benefic, this transfer brings a change of location and cosmic alignment towards things set down in the foundation chart. They will come back around to previous anomalous situations involving full payments. If there is a diameter, punishments and oppositions will occur.

Mars to Venus brings hatred, separations from female figures, instability at home, death to the mother (for those who have them in feminine signs), intimacy, fights over transience, and displays of affection. If they have sympathy, the native will survive the cold though an instability to the praxis. Women will come into bloody situations such as miscarriage. They will pass through the danger.

Mars to Mercury indicates a tumultuous, transitional year. There will be danger, fines, joy through writing, money, and counting. There will be controversy over the mysteries, a nearness to evil works, depravation, increased burdens, and defensive speeches. When in double-bodied signs, with similar manifestations indicated in other places, they will be quite rogue, acting thoughtlessly or recklessly. If the three aphetic points are safe, they will be surrounded by things mentioned earlier. If poorly configured, there will be instability in the accomplishments. If configured righteously, indications will be weakened. Natives will survive increased responsibilities and diversions from those they encounter.

κγ; The Distribution of Years of Venus

Venus giving over to itself in finer divisions, when well placed, leads to friendliness, collaborations, sympathy with both males and females, gifts, pleasant intimate experiences, delightful marriage, goodwill, kindness at home, pleasure, and help. If with Saturn or Mars, gazed upon by them, or in unproductive signs, then blame, spectacles, fights, fines, rejection, judgements by female servants, and anarchy. It is the same to women from men.

Venus to the Sun brings about a reputable and abundant time for introductions to both male and female characters, help through intimacy, marriage, children, purchasing, cosmic and bodily gifts, a good reputation to the father, and sympathies or assistance through these affairs; even more so when well-configured. To those in elevated positions, there will be awards such as wreaths and chaplets. It leads to priesthood, advancement, leadership, productive gifts within the crowds, mystical writings, sharing in the stories of the gods, aphrodisial affairs, mirth, and merriment.

Venus to the Moon, lying beautifully, configured to acquire resources in timely places, indicate a helpful period, a cosmic alignment and visions about the livelihood, a notable reputation (along with jealous anger), a love of contention, victory, stand-offs, and malicious secrets. This will lead to un-manifested acquisitions and help, as determined by the allotted portions. When configured poorly, this will create unrighteous behavior and hatred from male and female characters both. There will be elevation and instability among kin and friendly characters. There will be rivalry, a love of contention and victory, and transfer of these things in general.

Venus to Saturn indicates a prominent, harmful period, separations from women over fights, and hubris. It leads to displays of unrighteousness and hatred towards the mother, women, and kin. Dishonor with older characters and blame among the common people. A divided logic will also be present. This is encompassed by ugly, shameful experiences, and instability with intimacy and loved ones. There will be lawsuits involving a woman, and a remaining in the location during and throughout confrontations. It creates a cooling off of practical affairs, weakness, the discovery of secrets, the formation of great plans through toil in the *aistheterion*, insults, disparaging remarks, drug use, potions (pharmaceuticals, etc.), pathologies that linger for a certain time period, more so when Mars or Mercury share in the aspect configuration.

Venus to Jupiter indicates a good and abundant year, and a coming together with people of a higher social reputation. It leads to gifts, leadership, political affairs, visions of a good reputation among the crowd, advancement into marriage, counsel and deliberation with female characters, conception among friends, children, and aphrodisial relationships in areas of which the native partakes. If the chart is somehow mediocre, this time will be good for work; releasing the native from paltry, ordinary tasks and subservient roles, as there will be belief. This time will draw down a worthiness and honor. A cosmic alignment to foundation and all it represents.

Venus to Mars, will elevate the year. There will be fights and separations with women, bloodshed, envy, ill will with females, death to the mother, lawsuits because of women, rivalry, survival through hatred, displays of fault and blame, and adultery. There can be errors in judgement and advanced payment, passing through the fortunes that are alongside the deliberate course of action. Those using the art of speaking and delivery will be carried into correction, being chastised and the like. This kind of thing can bring special prayers and invocations for the separation of partnership, those leading themselves to hold fast on the hopes and dreams, and the persisting of senseless chatter about expectations for the future, resulting in notorious scandals.

Venus to Mercury indicates a practical and shrewd time and intelligence about what has been cast. It is indicative of giving and receiving, commerce over logic and education, making the rounds with budding friends, the purchasing of cosmic wares in the marketplace, wedlock with men or women, a good reputation, honor, straightforward practical affairs, learning a great deal about the mysteries, handling things entrusted (deposits, etc.), belief, and sympathies with kin.

κδ; The Finer Distributions of Mercury

Mercury giving over to itself in the finer divisions is practical and helpful for fully manifesting the tasks attempted. This transfer is also good for the beliefs and shrewd intelligence, enmity among superiors, public and secret speeches, accomplishing business in a straightforward manner, spending days cheerfully, doing logical tasks, or counting. If rising in the east, in productive signs, looked on by Jupiter and Venus, this indicates greater faith and more help. Witnessed by malefics, fear and contradictions will result.

Mercury handing over to Sun creates a year that hits the mark, bringing common awareness to the praxis, commendations by greats, responsibilities, and gifts, along with delays, obstacles, etc. Great inheritance, authority, sharing in the stories of mystical works, conjecture and new ideas about education. From a logical standpoint, help will also manifest. In most cases things will manifest mysteriously. The native is surrounded, putting on a show.

Mercury handing over to Moon signifies a practical year, especially if configured well; the Moon rising up in the east, also in a productive placement, will lead to collaborations with both female and male characters, aid through business, straightforward beliefs, effective accomplishments, and a sympathetic nature to those with a greater social visage. If configured in alien houses and looked on by malefics, judgements, payments, abusive threats, and boastful promises by greater individuals will result, leading to oppression or fear through the mysteries, and abandonment.

Mercury to Saturn signifies a year of upheaval and dangerous situations, the dismantling of business, spiteful punishments, judgements, rejoicing through writings and the mysteries, weakness, illness, wasting away and disturbances from bile. Also, taking the hand to pharmaceuticals, witnessing death (by his own kind, brothers, or children), and judgements and controversy surrounding death. Suppose they are in a mean position (by the oppositions or square), in the gaze of Mars. According to these configurations, the native could experience danger through something they are building, or a shipwreck could manifest. He could pass time by rolling around with those he encounters, causing anguish. When configured well by house — payments, an elevated reputation, and straightforward practical affairs are the result. When turned away, this will bring average, mediocre manifestations.

Mercury to Jupiter leads to a practical time, collaborations with shrewd individuals, friendliness, straightforward practical affairs, inheritance, powers of divination, and prosperity through logic and counting. Bewilderment in the crowd, scandal, survival through untimely and unnerving things, collapse into argument over payments, instability at home and with friends, survival through physical agony, and not putting one's own needs above others.

Mercury to Mars is not good. This transfer brings hatred, judgements, punishment, evil works, counterfeit writing, forgery, pledges, loans, increased burdens, plundering, instability, abandonment, scheming, slaughter, and anarchy at home. This can especially be true when these things are indicated elsewhere. Natives become quite practical yet also very complicated. They construct and build things and make amends for ideas or points of view. They pass through tumultuous situations, responsibilities, and expectations; hopes and plans are subjugated.

Mercury to Venus signifies a good and practical time, fit for trading in the marketplace, contracts in aphrodisial affairs, help through inheritance, logic, education, collaboration, acquiring friends, new intimacy, and being diverted through such intertwinings with men and women. For those in greater positions, this will set down influences for the body and lead to cosmic acquisitions, responsibilities, friendships, advancements into good positions, and good energy towards one's own.

κε; The Distribution of the Four Lots

The lot of fortune handing over or receiving in a productive place, with benefics on or witnessing it, indicates good luck, advancement of praxis, and reputation. The practical affairs will be straightforward, providing consummate manifestation of what is expected, and aid from affairs of the dead. If the lot has declined, witnessed by malefics, this will provide weakness to the praxis, reputation, and transient situations. As much as can be accomplished with oppositions, danger, judgements, and threats.

The lot of spirit handing over or receiving in productive places, benefics on it, will bring about a clear plan of action for what the heart is set on — criticisms, straightforward logic in calculations, contracts and counsel from friends, help through collaborations, gifts from great people, and a good reputation. In terms of point of view, the native can easily hit the mark; being puffed up by great thoughts, intentions, and purpose. If fallen aside, witnessed by malefics, elevation through tests of spirit, lack of sensory perception, oppositions to what is cast, missing the mark at straightforward allotments, being carried into responsibilities for other people, and mistakes in the greatest way. From this, these people become faint hearted. It becomes dangerous for them to build something. It's as if they become frantic and mad through the reception, leading to a distracted heart and mind; bringing terror, astonishment, anger, etc.

The lot of eros handing over or receiving in productive places, benefics witnessing it, prepares the native for a moral purpose; to set his heart on, long for, covet, and desire something beautiful. For those in education, bodily professions, or music, things will turn around. Those taken to flattery will delight in hoping for what is to come, which leads to untiring distress. For the lovers, enchanted with intimacy and intercourse, it leads to good fortune from both men and women. When Mars and Mercury are also witnessing this place, or are on it, especially in their own signs, there will be a love of boys. If they are blemished in both places, a love of arms, the chase, and the *palaestra*[14]. If Venus, there will be intimacy

---

[14] *palaestra* = wrestling school, school (1291)

with females. In those that feel affection, there will be much support. Similarly, each of the stars when allotted to this place, witnessing it, and taking over for a time, will prepare the passions of heart for a certain image and form, consistent with its own particular nature. In general, when malefics are on these places, or witnessing, the passions will involve trials, punishments, and danger. If somehow Saturn is with Venus, also together with the Moon, or witnessing her, there will be ugly, shameful, and brutal works; finding fault with men and women, surviving scandals, changing one's mind, being converted, or conquered by pathology. If the star of Jupiter is somehow sharing the configuration, there will be credible, powerful, mystical occurrences. Mars and Mercury on these places, witnessing them, taking over the time period, bring evil work to the business affairs, and a love of piracy and plundering. Those engaging in forgery, counterfeit writings, burglary, playing dice, etc. (having the mind of a wild beast) will be seized. If the star of Venus is also configured, he will take his hand to drugs, and commit adultery. According to the time periods cast, there will be pledges and loans, rolling around with those who do evil works, oppression, and judgement, as they take their hand to dangerous tasks. A thing such as this would come about though the combined strength and placement of many factors; all of which must be considered. The lot of eros, in the day, is taken from fortune to spirit, and an equal interval from the ascendant; at night, the reverse.

The lot of necessity, handing over or receiving in productive places, benefics on or witnessing, leads to affinities, familiarities, and collaborations with greats, drawn down by hatred or death. When malefics are on its place, this will lead to adversaries, contention, judgements, and payments. From which, tasks will be followed through on and accomplished grievously, alongside the deliberate course of action. If the configuration is maltreated, the native could get a sentence or be overthrown. Take this calculation from spirit to fortune and the opposite way at night.

In the charts of men, things have been distinguished by time periods. Depending on the configuration and house layout, the transfer has potential to be fine tuned. The same is true in charts of females.

κς; The Distribution of Quarter Periods

And the Carrying Up of the Hepta-Zones, According to Critodemus.

Moon 1	1 year
Mercury 2	2 years
Venus 3	3 years
Sun 4	4 years
Mars 5	5 years
Jupiter 6	6 years
Saturn 7	7 years

This becomes 28.

The *mono-moiria* is taken as follows[15].

The Moon's sign will become the first ruler and will receive. The others are taken according to *zones*[16]. For instance, let us rejoice in an example where the Moon is at 6 Libra. The first star to receive will be

---

[15] *Mono-Moiria* = distribution of planets to each degree of the zodiac. Graduated by single degrees (1145).

[16] *zone* = belt, girdle, belt, waist, anything that goes round like a belt, one of the zones of the terrestrial sphere, planetary spheres (759)

Venus, second Mercury, third the Moon, fourth Saturn, fifth Jupiter, and sixth Mars.

Mars will become the *mono-moiria*.

Mars will receive first. The ruler of the *mono-moiria* of the Moon is 5 years. Then stars lying in succession, according to genesis, with Mars. When the filling up of years is 28, begin again from the star lying with Mars. This makes 10 years and 9 months. In daytime from the Sun, in nighttime from Moon. If the Sun is badly placed in a day chart, begin from the Moon. In a similar situation in a night chart, begin from Sun. If Sun and Moon are not dominant, then from the house ruler, or another well placed star.

κζ; Another from Seth Regarding the Yearly Cycles from Hermes

And, Making a Leisurely Aphesis from the Sun, Moon, Ascendant, and Lot of Fortune

There are four places from which the beginning of the year is taken; the Sun, Moon, ascendant, or fortune. The judgement goes as follows. The Sun on a pivot means we count from the Sun. At night, from the Moon on a pivot, by degree. These will later be taken from the ascendant. If the lot of fortune is on a pivot, and the lights are later, the beginning from it will indicate the quality of the year. A similar situation occurs when things are carried to the lights, on pivots, and they have begun from places other than their own sect. You will know that this teaching is stronger than our teaching, if the year is used to carry into parts of the genesis, through activities of a nature that matches the zodiacal signs involved. In the daytime cast from the Sun, if rising or near the midheaven. If not, cast out from the sign on the ascendant. The year in which the counting stops, from the ruler of the place from which the year was cast out in genesis. At night, cast from the Moon, if configured as mentioned before per the Sun, especially if rising in the east, and additive in numbers. In terms of life breathe of the two lights, if the numbers happen to not be filling up, but are instead getting smaller, then from the *sundesmon[17]*. (And if the things on the pivots are lying in greatness.) If it is exactly as has been written before, cast from the ruler of the place where counting stops from ascendant. If you discover signs on the pivots, benefic influences, or things to blame from stars present there, overseeing in the first arrangement and roadway around, this indicates beautiful outcomes in those years. Things walking opposite and far away from these places (such as stars making eastern risings and appearances), overseeing, and furnishing the praxis. Stars setting are impractical in that they diminish the fortune of experience, unless the practical tasks are hidden or clandestine.

---

[17] **Sundesmos** = that which binds together, bond of union, fastening. In grammar, a conjunction.

Conspiracy. In astronomy—node. In astrology—connection of heavenly bodies (1701).

κη; On What Kind of Month it Will Be

The month will be determined as follows. Take from
the transient Sun to the natal Sun, and an equal
interval from the sign allotted to the yearly cycle.
Look out for the sign in which the new moon
occurred, and also see if the genesis itself is synodic
— meaning it is a "new moon chart." Then, notice
the sign in which the full moon will occur, and
whether or not the natal chart is a full moon chart.
In these signs, the months will be productive; these
two places are beginnings. Then look to see what
condition has been laid down in genesis. Is the Moon
traveling from its new moon phase, or its full moon
phase? Is the filling up happening on a similar place,
equal in force, etc.? What is the quality of the
month? For instance, if the new moon or full moon
occurs on the third or fifth day, then it will follow
that the beginning of the month is calculated for that
day.

κθ; On the Productive Days

The productive days are found as follows.

1. Multiply the full years set down in genesis by 5 1/4.

2. Add the multiplied number with the interval from;

Birth Date to Day of Inquiry.

3. According to Alexandria, add the intercalated days, which indicate the filling up of 1/4 years.

4. Cast this number out into all possible signs by 12.

5. Multiply the remainder by 5.

6. Count the number from birth date to inquiry year.

7. Make the division into 12.

8. Cast out the remaining number from Moon through genesis, counting one on each sign.

9. From the sign allotted, cast out the month.

10. If you arrive at that number, scope out the ruler of that sign and any stars on it. Observe what sort of nature is indicated on those days.

***

The hours are taken as follows. From the allotted sign, cast out during the day, near the day's beginning, in two hour increments from the birth hour. You will discover beautiful, practical hours. These hours will be positive and useful for all pragmatic affairs cast in the chart.

Also, take note of the *Katarche*[18].

You can especially know the weak hours and *kataklitic*[19] moments by calculating the hours accurately from ascendant degree to the lights, and the various pivots of the stars.

---

[18] ***Kat-Arche*** = beginning, forecast of an undertaking or voyage, primacy, starting point (910)

[19] ***Kata-Klisis*** = making one lie down, seating him at a table, the taking to bed, a certain kind of lying down, lay prostrate. In Astrology, a horoscope cast at the hour when a patient takes to his bed (894)

Many have authority on this speculation, as they have done great preparation, building credibility to speak on the matter. Much has been lost by these books being reduced, meaning any extra information is also a great contribution. If a person's complexion is good, the spirit will naturally be well-formed, and the mind innately guided to arithmetic and calculations. Then he will take on the leadership to do so in a natural way.

When making the walk up and down, use the star-boundaries of 8, 7, 6, 5, and 4, if the year is from the Sun. Or if the month is taken from the Sun, by its roadway around to Moon in genesis, and the same interval from ascendant. I also observe the yearly cycles as laid out by Hermes. Make the aphesis and the roadway around, from all stars to all stars by the ascensional times of the signs, according to the various *klima* regions. For instance, if inquiring about a woman through Venus, this can manifest in the form of daughters or feminine characters; when inquiring about praxis, from Mercury. Look to the connections it makes. When inquiring about danger, death, illness, or bloodshed, look for malefics on the ascendant, Sun, or Moon.

Other topics are handled similarly.

The stars must make their way around, walking through certain bounds, having various, unique rays cast on them by other stars. At times, a star will trample along in the sign of another star, also making its way around. Moreover, in the transfer and reception process, natal potentials are drawn and flushed out by an increase in intensity. In this way, a thing in the birth chart will literally manifest. There is more to consider on the yearly cycle. The yearly period is taken from the Sun, which indicates matters of soul and spirit. Also from the Moon, indicating bodily matters and mothers. We must also consider the Lot of Fortune. One must scrutinize these influences closely, to see their configurations to one another. If benefics are making harmonious appearances, this signifies a good year. If malefics, the opposite. If both benefics and malefics, the year's manifestations will form a mixture. We must use all things mentioned about the years in relation to the dog-star, *Kunos*.

λ; The Practical & Impractical Times of Life, According to the Quarter Calculation of the Planetary Periods

Let us discuss the distribution of practical times according to the quarters.

Saturn's period is 30 years, 1/4 of which is 7 1/2.
Jupiter's period is 12 years, 1/4 of which is 3.
Mars is 15 years, 1/4 of which is 3 years, 9 months.
Sun is 19 years, 1/4 of which is 4 years, 9 months.
Venus is 8 years, 1/4 of which is 2 years.
Mercury is 20 years, 1/4 of which is 5 years.
Moon is 25 years, 1/4 of which is 6 years, 3 months.

These are the micro-circles of the stars.

The greater circles come out as follows.

Sun is 120, Moon 108, Saturn 57,
Jupiter 79, Mars 66, Venus 82, Mercury 76.

The days are allotted as follows.

Saturn is 637, Jupiter 255, Mars 318, Sun 433, Venus 368 18, Mercury 423 18, Moon 531.

Jupiter from 3 years is allotted its own days of 102, Mars 127 12, Sun 161 6, Venus 67 12, Mercury 170 12, Moon 212 6, Saturn 255.

Mars from 3 years and 9 months gets its own 159 5, Saturn 318, Jupiter 127, Sun 219, Venus 84 18, Mercury 212 21, Moon 265 2/3.

Sun from 4 years and 9 months to Saturn 403, to Jupiter 161 12 hours, Mars 201, Sun 255 8, Venus 66 21, Mercury 267 4, Moon 336 6.

Venus year 2 to Saturn 170, to Jupiter 68, to Mars 85, Sun 107 12, to itself 45, to Mercury 113 12, to Moon 141 12.

Mercury year 5. To Saturn 425, Jupiter 170, Mars 212, Sun 268 17, Venus 112, itself 283 12, and Moon 358 18.

Moon from 6 years and 3 months to Saturn 425, to Jupiter 170, to Mars 265 15, to Sun 336, to Venus 141 16, to Moon 452.

From this one might set down at a certain year, the first ruler of the sign to give over. For instance, Saturn is 85, then Sun 53 and 18 hours, Mercury 56 and 18 hours, Venus 22 and 18 hours, Jupiter 34, Moon 70 and 18 hours, Mars 42 and 12 hours.

Examining the magnitude of star boundaries for any star in the twelve signs will give a certain number of years. Suppose the ascendant is Libra. The native is brought down at 28 years. Capricorn is given the first 57 years because of Saturn, then Mercury 76, Venus 82, Jupiter 79, Mars 65, Moon 70, and Sun 6 hours.

Let us observe another division. The minimal years of a star are multiplied by 4, giving 25 to the Moon and 6 years per the Sun. The star of Saturn will be next because of the 120 days of Capricorn, then Mercury 80, Venus 32, Jupiter 48, Mars 60, Moon 25, then Sun 6 hours.

The yearly ratio of day and night are derived from the ascendant. One is taken down at the 28th year, the minimal years from Libra. And yet Saturn to Taurus. And the 28th year sets down in Leo. In terms of Libra, Saturn has transferred over to the Sun, and the Sun has the year.

This would please the Egyptians,
Babylonians, and Greeks.

The triangles are combined by 28. Venus holds rulership of the triangle. From Venus in Cancer, the counting stops in Libra. The ruler of the triangle is Saturn in Libra. Saturn takes over the year from Venus. This distribution fights.

Appendix

TRIANGLE RULERS

	DAY BIRTH ☉	NIGHT BIRTH ☽
1. FIRE TRIANGLE ♈ ARIES ♐ SAGITTARIUS ♌ LEO	1. SUN ☉ 2. JUPITER ♃ 3. SATURN ♄	1. JUPITER ♃ 2. SUN ☉ 3. SATURN ♄
2. EARTH TRIANGLE ♑ CAPRICORN ♍ VIRGO ♉ TAURUS	1. VENUS ♀ 2. MOON ☽ 3. MARS ♂	1. MOON ☽ 2. VENUS ♀ 3. MARS ♂
3. AIR TRIANGLE ♒ AQUARIUS ♎ LIBRA ♊ GEMINI	1. SATURN ♄ 2. MERCURY ☿ 3. JUPITER ♃	1. MERCURY ☿ 2. SATURN ♄ 3. JUPITER ♃
4. WATER TRIANGLE ♏ SCORPIO ♓ PISCES ♋ CANCER	1. VENUS ♀ 2. MARS ♂ 3. MOON ☽	1. MARS ♂ 2. VENUS ♀ 3. MOON ☽

List of Roman Emperors

27 B.C. - 14	Augustus
14 - 37	Tiberius
37 - 41	Gaius
41 - 54	Claudius
54 - 68	Nero
69 - 79	Vespasian
79 - 81	Titus
81 - 96	Domitian
96 - 98	Nerva
98 - 117	Trajan
117 - 138	Hadrian
138 - 161	Antoninus Pius
161 - 192	Commodus
193 - 212	Septimius Severus
212 - 217	Antoninus Severus
217 - 218	Macrinus
218 - 222	Elagabalus
222 - 235	Severus Alexander
235 - 238	Maximinus
238 - 244	Gordian III
244 - 249	Philip the Arab

Egyptian months --- 30 days each

1 THOTH

2 PHAOPHI

3 ATHYR

4 CHOIAK

5 TYBI

6 MECHIR

7 PHAMENOTH

8 PHAMENOUTHI

9 PACHON

10 PAYNI

11 EPIPHI

12 MESORE

Works Cited

Brennan, Chris. *Hellenistic Astrology: The Study of Fate and Fortune.* Denver, CO: Amor Fati Publications, 2017.

Dilke, O.A.W. *Greek and Roman Maps.* Ithaca, NY: Cornell University Press, 1985.

Hand, Robert. *An Introduction to the "Anthology" of Vettius Valens.* From a translation by Robert Schmidt at Project Hindsight.

Kroll, Guilelmus. *Vettii Valentis: Anthologiarum Libri.* Berolini, 1908.

Liddell, Henry George and Robert Scott. *Greek-English Lexicon.* Clarendon Press, 1996.

Porphyry of Tyre. *A Writing from Galnos to Gauron Regarding the Manner in Which Embryos are Ensouled.* Greek Original. Critical Edition.

Porphyry of Tyre. *An Introduction to the Tetrabiblos of Ptolemy.* Trans. by Andrea L. Gehrz. Portland, Oregon: The Moira Press, 2010.

Vettius Valens. *Anthology, Book 2.1.* Gehrz translation. Moira Press: OR, 2016.

Ptolemy, Claudius. *Tetrabiblos.* Trans. by F.E. Robbins. Cambridge and London: Harvard University Press, 1940.

Riley, Mark. *Vettius Valens Anthology.* Available online.

Rey, H.A. Find the Constellations. Boston: Houghton Mifflin Harcourt, 2008.

Valens, Vettius. *Anthology.* Critical Edition by David Pingree. Leipzig: B.G. Teubner, 1986.

About the Editor

Sara Beth Brooks is an Astrologer and the editor for Moira Press. Brooks has a longstanding friendship and professional relationship with the translator

(Gehrz) and an especially deep love for the works of Vettius Valens. When not assisting Andrea with ancient texts, she can be found living as a renegade paranormal investigator, self-appointed steward of forgotten cemeteries, seeker of ghost towns, and general lover of obscurity and solitude.

Andrea L. Gehrz

Other Books by Moira Press

Vettius Valens of Antioch
(120-175 C.E.) Anthology: Book One

Topics include:

The Nature of the Wandering Stars

The Nature of the Twelve Constellations

The Star Boundaries within Each Constellation

The Hour of Birth

The Midheaven

The Ascensional Times of the Twelve Constellations

Calculating New moons and Full moons by Hand

The Masculine and Feminine Degrees

Calculating the Nodes by Hand

The Twining of the Qualities of the Planets

The Conception Chart

Pages: 254

Price: $29.95 (Amazon)

Vettius Valens Anthology: Book 2.1

Price: $19.95 @ Amazon.com

Vettius Valens Anthology: Book 2.1.2

In 2.1.2, part two of the second book in an epic nine book Anthology, ancient Greek astrologer Vettius Valens covers the following topics:

True and Complete Spiritual Happiness from Triplicities, Ascendant, Fortune, Exaltation Points of Sun and Moon, Lot of Spirit, and Eleventh Place from Fortune.

Remarkable Charts versus Dejected Ones

Many Examples

Price: $19.95 @ Amazon.com

Vettius Valens Anthology: Book 2.1.3

In the third installment of the second book of his nine book Anthology, ancient Greek astrologer Vettius Valens covers the following topics:

Practical and Impractical Times of Life
> Taken from the Pivots, and the Regions
> Carried Up to Them.

Life Abroad, from the Works of Hermippos.

On Life Abroad.

An Early End to Paretns.

And Another on Parents, from Timaeus.

Orphanhood from the Parents.

Separation from the Parents.

Freedom and Enslavement in Nativities.

The Eleven Configurations of the Moon.

Injuries and Pathologies.

Marriage; The Luxuries of Joining Together.

A Holistic Viewing of Many Schematics.

Life With and Without Children.

Siblings.

Violent Death.

Price: $19.95 @ amazon.com

Vettius Valens Anthology: Book 3.1

In Book 3, Valens covers:

Supreme and Ultimate Rulership
Significant Degrees
Reckoning the Vital Quadrant
Winds
Steps
Exaltations
Classification
Useful Time Periods
Climax Points

Price: $19.95 @ amazon.com

Porphyry of Tyre (234-305 C.E.)

An Introduction to the Tetrabiblos

Originally written in ancient Greek by the philosopher Porphyry of Tyre, this textbook sets out the basics of ancient astrological theory. It is a perfect introduction to traditional astrology, as it is simple, elegant, and technical. Topics include:

Ancient Beam Theory, Apogee and Perigee
Nocturnal and Diurnal Planets
Sign Rulerships, Exaltations
The Casting of Planetary Rays
The Body Parts associated with the Twelve Signs
The Productive Places, Conception
Conception, Masculine and Feminine Signs
Ascensional Times of the Signs
Fixed Stars, Etc.

Pages: 72 $16.95 on Amazon.com

Porphyry of Tyre; Ensoulment

"Gehrz breathes delicate new life into this ancient text, unfolding the threads of Porphyry's thoughts anew. Fundamental questions for astrology—When does the soul move into the body? Where does the soul come from? — are considered methodically from myriad angles and potentials. This text is an enlivening read for anyone exploring the roots of astrology from historical, philosophical, and ontological perspectives." Jenn Zahrt, PhD

Astrological Remediation:
A Guide for the Modern Practitioner

This book is invaluable for any practicing astrologer, as it teaches the art of healing challenges in the chart. Whether clients are approaching a hard transit or examining a natal struggle, this book can help. Topics include astrology and medicine, astrological diagnosis, isolating planets that need remedies, working with children, the tenets of astral mechanics as written by Judith Hill, and more.

Strategic Planning
Symbolic Substitution
Vibrational Merging
Astrally-Timed Information

$29.95 @ amazon.com

A Wonderbook of True Astrological Case Files

In this magical book of astral tales, Judith Hill and Andrea Gehrz team up to bring astrology to the world! Each story is a simple yet eloquent example of the wonderful light science of astrology. The Wonderbook contains over 50 stories of animals with birth times, medical anomalies, holly bus drivers, love contracts, tiny nooks, and much much more.

Story titles include:

The Skeptic
The Ossified Man
Astro Twins
Sky Rocks
Stellar Rescue
The Strange Request
The Cosmic Microscope
Manifest Destiny
And More!

Price: $16.95 on Amazon